EFFECTIVE TEACHING

What is effective teaching?

In the nineteenth century, teacher training institutions were called 'normal schools' because it was assumed there was only one way to teach – the 'norm'. Today there is no single style of teaching endorsed by everyone. How teachers teach depends on factors like the age and ability of the children, their background and needs, the nature of the subject or topic being studied and the resources available.

The authors draw on their considerable experience of teacher training and research into classrooms, to explore several dimensions of teaching. These include planning and preparation, direct instruction, the management of materials and of behaviour, conversation with children, monitoring, and evaluating learning. They show how teachers can improve their competence and meet their aspirations, both individually and with their colleagues. The book will be very useful to trainee and experienced teachers, heads, teacher trainers and inspectors.

Richard Dunne is a Lecturer in the School of Education at Exeter University.

Ted Wragg is Professor of Education at Exeter University and is the author of many books including, in this series, *Class Management* and with George Brown, *Explaining* and *Questioning*. He writes a regular column for the *Times Educational Supplement* and is a frequent commentator for radio and television on education matters.

LEVERHULME PRIMARY PROJECT

The Leverhulme Project, based at Exeter University, directed by Ted Wragg and Neville Bennett and coordinated by Clive Carré, was a major survey of primary teacher education since 1988. Its bank of valuable information about what actually happens in classrooms and how teachers are reacting to current changes in education will be used for a variety of publications including the *Classroom Skills* series.

All primary teachers need to master certain basic pedagogical skills. This set of innovative yet practical resource books for teachers covers each of those skills in turn. Each book contains

- Practical, written and oral activities for individual and group use at all stages of professional development
- Transcripts of classroom conversation and teacher feedback and photographs of classroom practice to stimulate discussion
- Succinct and practical explanatory text

Other titles in the series

TALKING AND LEARNING IN GROUPS	*Elisabeth Dunne and Neville Bennett*
CLASS MANAGEMENT	*E.C. Wragg*
EXPLAINING	*E.C. Wragg and George Brown*
QUESTIONING	*George Brown and E.C. Wragg*

Leverhulme Primary Project ■ Classroom Skills Series

Series editor
Clive Carré

EFFECTIVE TEACHING

Richard Dunne and Ted Wragg

London and New York

First published 1994
by Routledge
11 New Fetter Lane, London EC4P 4EE

Simultaneously published in the USA and Canada
by Routledge
29 West 35th Street, New York, NY 10001

Transferred to Digital Printing 2003

Typeset in Palatino by
Selwood Systems, Midsomer Norton
Printed and bound in Great Britain by
Biddles Short Run Books, King's Lynn

British Library Cataloguing in Publication Data

A catalogue record for this book is available from the British
Library

Library of Congress Cataloging in Publication Data

A catalog record for this book has been requested

ISBN 0-415-10916-7

CONTENTS

PREFACE

Improving the quality of what happens in primary school and preparing children for life in the twenty-first century requires the highest quality of professional training. The Leverhulme Primary Project *Classroom Skills* series and its companion series *Curriculum in Primary Practice* are designed to assist in this training.

The Leverhulme Primary Project *Classroom Skills* focuses on the essential classroom competences. It explores the classroom strategies available to teachers and the patterns of classroom organisation which best assist pupil learning. Throughout, it demonstrates that at the very heart of teacher education is the ability to make sense of what is going on in the classroom. This series of books is based on the research of the Leverhulme Primary Project, a three-year programme of research into various aspects of primary teacher education, funded by the Leverhulme Trust and carried out at the University of Exeter. The companion series, *Curriculum in Primary Practice*, helps teachers to make judgements and devise strategies for teaching particular subjects.

Both series are designed to assist teachers at all stages of their professional development. They will be useful for:

- practising teachers
- student teachers
- college and university tutors
- school-based in-service coordinators
- advisory teachers
- school mentors and headteachers

This book can be used as part of initial training or in in-service programmes in school. The text can also be read by individuals as a source of ideas and it will be helpful in teacher appraisal as an aid to developing professional awareness both for those being appraised and for the appraisers. Like all the books in both series, *Effective Teaching* contains suggested activities which have been tried out by teachers and those in pre-service training and revised in the light of their comments.

We hope that both series will provoke discussion, help you to reflect on your current practice and encourage you to ask questions about everyday classroom events.

Clive Carré
University of Exeter

AIMS AND CONTENTS

Effective teaching lies at the very heart of the effective school. What it is and how to nurture it is something we try to explore in this book, but whatever one's notions of what constitutes 'effective' teaching, few would doubt that it is essential if schools are to flourish. What is more important, however, is that time spent not only improving the quality of what each individual teacher does, but also the effectiveness of the whole school, is a wise investment.

The major aim of this book, therefore, is to help both newcomers and experienced professionals gain further insights into their own teaching and that of others. Teaching is a set of craft skills, values, beliefs and practices that can be added to and improved at all stages even of a long career. There are teachers close to retirement who are still willing to innovate, to look closely at what they do in the classroom, at what their pupils learn, and to reflect alone or with others on how to improve their practice.

The intention is that, by reading the text and trying out some of the practical activities, teachers will be able to improve their own classroom practice. If people work together as a group, whether they are experienced teachers in the same school, tutors and student trainees on an initial training programme, or some combination of these, then this will be even better. The emphasis is on both activity and reflection, for one without the other would be less effective. All the activities can be done by individuals or by groups of students or experienced teachers, either in discussion or with children on their own or in someone else's classroom. The use of jargon is minimised, though not omitted entirely, as from time to time it can help to have a specific term that covers some key concept.

The book is organised in the following six units:

In **Unit 1** there is consideration of what constitutes effective teaching.

Unit 2 describes an approach to teaching based on nine dimensions of classroom practice at different levels of competence, as well as a framework for discussing teaching.

Unit 3 explores how children learn and how teachers can plan teaching strategies to meet their needs.

Unit 4 deals with classroom organisation and management.

Unit 5 concentrates on instructional design and how teachers' subject knowledge, understanding of children, beliefs and statutory obligations affect it.

Unit 6 looks at whole-school issues and how teachers in a school can plan and secure minor or radical changes.

There is no favouring of a single approach to teaching, therefore, even though we often put forward models we have ourselves developed. The emphasis is on teachers exploring the issues, considering alternatives, trying out ideas and then finding their own best way forward in the light of their own experience and that of others.

How to use this book

The six units constitute substantial course material in the field of effective teaching. The activities and text are suitable for in-service and professional studies courses as well as for individual use.

The *text* may be read as a book in its own right; all the *activities* can be undertaken either by individual teachers or by members of a group working together on the topic. The *discussion activities* are intended to be worked on individually but also lend themselves to group discussion when completed. The *practical activities* are designed to be done in the teacher's own classroom or by student teachers on teaching practice or when they are teaching children brought into the training institution for professional work.

The book can either be used alone or in conjunction with other books in the Classroom Skills series. For example, the management of small groups is not covered in great detail because the book by Elisabeth Dunne and Neville Bennett, *Talking and Learning in Groups*, in the Classroom Skills series covers the topic much more fully. Class management, questioning and explaining are all covered in separate volumes in this same series.

Those responsible for courses, therefore, may well wish to put together exercises and activities from several of the books in this series to make up their own course as part of a general professional skills development programme, either in initial training or of whole-school professional development.

Usually the discussion and written activities described will occupy between 1 and $1\frac{1}{2}$ hours and classroom activities may be completed in about half an hour, though this may vary, depending on the context.

The following symbols are used throughout the book to denote:

quotations from published materials

activities

transcripts of children or teachers talking during lessons

WHAT IS EFFECTIVE TEACHING?

Although it is not always easy to define exactly what different people might mean by the term 'effective', teachers have always needed a wide range of subject knowledge and a large repertoire of professional skills. Teaching young children to read and write, to understand the world around them, to grasp and be able to apply fundamental mathematical and scientific principles, to use their developing intelligence and imagination, to live and work harmoniously with others, all require an effective teacher to possess knowledge and understanding of the content of the subjects and topics being taught, as well as the ability to manage a class, explain clearly, ask intelligent and appropriate questions, and monitor and assess learning.

There are many factors which combine to demand from teachers ever higher levels of professional competence. These include the rapid growth in the acquisition of knowledge, the changing nature not only of adult employment, but also of recreation and leisure, the increased public pressure for accountability, the development of new forms of educational and information technology, and the broadening role of the primary teacher. In combination they represent an overwhelming pressure for improvement by all practitioners, even the many who already manifest a high degree of skill in the classroom.

In the nineteenth century, teacher training institutions were known as 'normal schools', on the grounds that there was some single 'norm' endorsed by society. Today the factors mentioned above require levels of skill, understanding, imagination, and resilience from teachers which go infinitely beyond the rudimentary common sense and mechanical competence fostered by the normal schools of the last century.

The implications for teachers are clear. There is so much to know and understand, so if you cannot know everything, you must know something. Hence the many efforts made either at regional or national level to determine the *content* of education – what children of a particular age or level of ability ought to learn – or by teachers themselves at local level to shape and implement a coherent curriculum. Secondly, if you cannot know or learn everything, you must be able to find out for yourself, and this is why the *process* of learning has become important, as well as, though not instead of, the content. Thirdly, since their pupils can acquire only a tiny fraction of the knowledge and skills currently available to humanity, teachers must develop teaching strategies which not only transmit information, but also encourage children to learn independently and as a member of a group.

Citizens in the twenty-first century are more likely to be willing to learn throughout their lives if they have been fired and enthused, rather than rebuffed and demoralised in school. The quality of personal relationships between teacher and taught, therefore, is a direct result of the interpersonal skills of the teacher, who usually sets the tone in a class, or has to take the initiative to improve relationships should they go awry. A notion of effective teaching that embraced only the transmission of knowledge would be a poor one in such a context.

Furthermore in the twenty-first century many people will work in service industries, and others will run small businesses. This shift out of the factory and into closer contact with people, rather than machinery, requires a high degree of imagination, inventiveness, drive and interpersonal skills. Again a sound basis for those qualities can be established in good primary schools, and teachers who nurture them should be greatly valued.

The teacher attempting to teach the topic 'Insects'

to a primary class fifty years ago would not have been compared with anyone other than another teacher. Today she will be compared with the finest television presenters in the world, whose programmes on insects enjoy multi-million pound budgets and access to the very best of wildlife film available. Even if the quality of teaching improves, it may not improve far or fast enough to match the escalating demands on teachers.

The public debate about teaching effectiveness has too often been over-simplified and caricatured as 'traditional' versus 'progressive', 'formal' versus 'informal', 'phonics' versus 'real books', when the reality of classroom life is that many teachers prefer to use a mixture of methods rather than fill out a single stereotype. In the workbooks on professional skills which we have produced during the Leverhulme Primary Project, such as *Class Management* (Wragg 1993), *Questioning* (Brown and Wragg 1993) and *Explaining* (Wragg and Brown 1993), trainee and experienced teachers are encouraged to analyse and determine their own teaching strategies, rather than merely copy someone else's preferences.

There is less dissent about what constitutes effective teaching in discussion between people outside the profession than there is in the research and evaluation literature. Good teachers, it is commonly held, are keen and enthusiastic, well organised, firm but fair, stimulating, know their stuff, and are interested in the welfare of their pupils. Few would attempt to defend the converse: that good teachers are unenthusiastic, boring, unfair, ignorant, and do not care about their pupils.

Once the scrutiny of teaching is translated into the more precise terms demanded by the tenets of rigorous systematic enquiry, the easy agreement of casual conversation evaporates. Biddle and Ellena (1964), reporting the Kansas City role studies, found that there was not even clear agreement amongst teachers, parents and administrators about the role teachers should play. However, it is nonetheless well worth considering what appear to be the *outcomes* of teaching. If a school is effective, then probably most or all the teachers who work in it will be effective also. This raises questions, therefore, like 'What do children actually learn?' and 'What do teachers do that appears to help pupils to learn?'

ACTIVITY 1

1 As an individual or member of a group, write down a list of things that you hope children will learn in your class/school.

2 Look at your own list and put alongside it a word or two which you feel describes the category of learning involved, e.g. 'Children enjoy coming to school' (emotions), 'Children learn to read a range of books' (reading/language/knowledge), 'children learn to wait their turn, share and be a positive member of a group' (relationships/social behaviour).

3 Compare your list with those of others, if possible. Are there common features, or do you disagree amongst yourselves? If so, about what?

4 Select one or two areas where there seems to be some agreement about importance and discuss what individual teachers and the staff as a whole can do to improve effectiveness in these fields.

In the 1970s and 1980s some of the attempts to find a consensus in the research literature were criticised. For example, Gage (1978), summarising research studies which had attempted to relate what teachers did to what pupils actually learned, concluded that in the early years of schooling certain kinds of teacher behaviour did show some consistent relationship to children learning reading and arithmetic. From this he derived a set of prescriptive 'Teacher should' statements like 'Teachers should call on a child by name before asking the question', 'Teachers should keep to a minimum such activities as giving directions and organising the class for instruction', or 'During reading-group instruction, teachers should give a maximal amount of brief feedback and provide fast-paced activities of the "drill" type.'

Among the criticism of prescriptions based on summaries of recent findings are: the proposition that much American work in particular is based on short-term tests of memory; that formal didactic styles of teaching often show up better on short-term measures and could, therefore, easily be perpetuated; that the 'gains' of method A compared with method B are often slight. This last argument is skilfully countered by Gage (1985) in his book *Hard Gains in the Soft Sciences*. He shows how significant policy decisions, in fields such as medicine and public health, are often made on a degree of statistical 'superiority' that would receive little attention in educational research. He quotes examples of trials of beta blockers and low cholesterol diets to reduce the incidence of heart attacks, which showed only 2.5 and 1.7 per cent differences respectively between experimental and control groups' mortality rates, but which nonetheless led to significant changes in public health policy and practice.

Teachers are compared with the finest television presentation

Doyle (1978) observed that reviewers of research into teacher effectiveness 'have concluded, with remarkable regularity, that few consistent relationships between teacher variables and effectiveness can be established'. The difficulty of identifying and evaluating teaching skills and their effectiveness is neatly illustrated by an interesting experiment at the University of Michigan. Guetzkow *et al.* (1954) divided first-year students on a general psychology course into three groups. The first group was given a formal lecture course with regular tests, the second and third groups took part in tutorials and discussions. At the end of the course the lecture group out-performed the tutorial discussion groups on the final examination, and the course was also more favourably rated by the students. So far, this represents a victory for lecturing and testing on two commonly used criteria: test performance and student appraisal.

The investigators discovered, however, that the students in the discussion groups scored significantly higher than the lecture groups on a measure of interest in psychology, the subject being studied. They hypothesised that though the lecture-group students gave a favourable rating of the teaching they had received, this may have been because they had less anxiety about grades for the course through their weekly feedback from test scores. It was decided to monitor the subsequent progress of all the groups. Three years later not one student in the lecture group had opted to study the subject further, but fourteen members of the two discussion and tutorial groups had chosen to major in psychology. Thus, on short-term criteria the lecture method was superior, but taking a longer perspective the discussion method appeared to motivate students more powerfully, and ultimately some must have learned a great deal more.

Defining effectiveness in such a way that all would agree, therefore, is not a simple matter. If we were to say that 'being effective' is, in practice, whatever teachers do to enable children to learn, then most people would rule out intimidation, humiliation, the use of corporal punishment or other forms of teacher behaviour of which they personally happen to disapprove. It is perhaps easier when seeking a definition to describe some of the characteristics of effective teaching which might

The excitement of learning

win some degree of consensus, though not universal agreement.

The first might be that the behaviour concerned 'facilitates pupils' learning of something worthwhile', such as facts, skills, values, concepts, how to live harmoniously with one's fellows, or some other outcome thought to be desirable. The notion of something being 'worthwhile' brings together both content and values in teaching. Skill is not a unidimensional concept. Teaching someone to steal might in one sense be skilfully done but it would attract professional odium rather than admiration. A second feature of effective teaching, therefore, is that the skill concerned is acknowledged to be a skill by those competent to judge, and this might include teachers, teacher trainers, inspectors, advisers and learners themselves.

For them to be a recognised part of a teacher's professional effectiveness, skills should also be capable of being repeated, not perhaps in exactly the same form, but as a fairly frequent rather than a single chance occurrence. A chimpanzee might randomly produce an attractive colourful shape once in a while, given a brush and some paint, but an artist would produce a skilfully conceived painting on a more regular basis. Teachers who possess professional skills, therefore, should be capable of manifesting these consistently, not on a hit-or-miss basis.

Uncertainty about the proper standing of the notion of effectiveness when applied to teaching is partly explained by the varied nature of the teacher's job. Pressing the right button on a tape recorder, or writing legibly on the blackboard, require but modest competence, and are things most people could learn with only a little practice. Responding to a disruptive 10-year old, or knowing how to explain a difficult concept to children of different ages and abilities by choosing the right language register, appropriate examples and analogies, and reading the many cues which signal understanding or bewilderment, require years of practice as well as considerable intelligence and insight.

When children learn something, there is often a magical quality about the excitement of discovery, the warmth of regard between teacher and taught, or the novelty to the learner of what is taking place, and the romanticism seems to be destroyed if teaching is seen as too deliberate, calculated, manipulated or over-analysed. However, it is possible for teachers, both individually and as a group of colleagues, to analyse what they are doing in a systematic way, and in the rest of this workbook we explore some of the ways of doing that.

IMPROVING PERSONAL COMPETENCE

The effective teacher needs a wide range of subject knowledge and a large repertoire of professional skills. When we made this statement in Unit 1 it served as a useful reminder of how complicated teaching is, but it still begs many questions. What does it mean, for example, for a primary teacher to 'know' a subject? There are difficult problems in specifying this. What a primary teacher can be expected to know about history must be very different from what a historian knows, and probably very different from what a secondary teacher knows. But what does a primary teacher *need* to know?

What constitutes professional skills? There have been many attempts to define these, but they are usually inadequate to describe what teachers actually do. In any case, if we were able to describe what knowledge and skills teachers require, we still need to work out how to help novices acquire them and how teachers make the most effective use of them. In every area of human activity it is the very skilled performance that makes things look simple. When we watch a skilled sportsperson make a mistake it is very easy to be critical about something we could not even begin to achieve. This is often the case when people see the work, or the results of the work, of a teacher.

It is also the case that skills need a lot of practice. This is accepted in most skilled activities, particularly sport and acting, but is less accepted in the case of teaching. Yet it is equally true of teaching. The problem is that while we are practising we are dealing with people, the children and parents, who care very much that teachers should already be effective.

The sort of complaint we might make about, say, an entertainer who does not quite succeed in an otherwise wonderfully skilled performance, is often made about teaching, perhaps about teaching children to read. There are sometimes complaints that teachers need to be more effective in this area and that they need to be taught this in initial training. Of course they should, and they usually are. The problem is that teaching a particular child to read means taking decisions that are sensitive and appropriate to the context. It is not just a case of selecting a set of materials for each 'type' of child: careful selections have continually to be made for individual children throughout their learning. It is precisely because effective teaching requires *interactive* decision making that it must be developed in real teaching situations.

If the teacher's job only involved teaching reading it would be demanding enough. It becomes even more so when we consider the full range of subjects that must be covered and the huge number of topics and skills and concepts within each one. If one sat down and worked out what this involves just to teach one single child, it would be formidable. Yet there is a further complication. Faced with a class of thirty children, teachers cannot replicate exactly what they would do when teaching just one child, nor can they just do it louder or do it thirty times. A class of children is sometimes best thought of as thirty individuals, but when teachers concentrate on an individual there are major problems of class management to be solved. In other contexts the class must be taught in quite different ways, raising problems of how most effectively to capitalise on the social nature of learning.

Improving personal competence in teaching involves thinking about how individual children might learn on their own, and how differently from this they learn in real classrooms. It also involves paying specific attention to the way the teacher works in the classroom, paying attention to the 'performance' of the teacher. We want to look at both of these aspects but begin in this unit with the question of performance. The word 'performance' has several meanings and connotations, and can arouse hostility if it is thought to suggest either an industrial model of maximising output, or playing to the gallery, or behaving in a mechanical, unthinking, uncritical manner. The term is used here simply as a shorthand for what teachers do in the classroom.

Focusing on classroom performance

The days have gone when teaching was seen as an individual and private process; it is now acknowledged that teachers benefit from working together, sharing ideas and discussing methods. A great deal of work of this type goes on in schools. It is quite usual to have team meetings and staff meetings as a normal part of professional life to improve the experience for the pupils. More and more work is being jointly planned and there is often some sort of team teaching going on. Governors and parents are also involved in the teaching in a variety of ways. These are welcome and important changes but may not be as beneficial as they might be.

One of the problems about collaborating with others to improve classroom work is that there is not a shared language about teaching. The introduction of the National Curriculum has provided some sort of shared language about curriculum (although we find this inadequate; see Unit 3) but this is different from the vocabulary that relates to classroom performance.

It is possible in teaching, as in all activities, to improve our own performance by carefully thinking about what we have done and how this might be improved. In teaching, it is often assumed that reflection is the most important way of increasing competence. It is quite common to talk about the need for teachers to be 'reflective' as if this is both easy and guaranteed to change how they act with children. We believe that in order to improve personal competence there is a need to work with one's colleagues. This process of a group of teachers stepping beyond reflection and into individual and collaborative action has been described by Wragg (1994) as being indicative of the 'dynamic school'.

It may sound obvious, and it is easy to claim that dynamic change is already common in schools. The telling question is what people need to do together as colleagues in order to improve significantly how they work in the classroom. It may be, of course, that talking about their work with others enhances their ability to think about what they are doing, and this is enough. We do not think that this is sufficient. We believe that learning from each other needs to include some sort of mentor relationship.

This does not mean merely teaming up with somebody who is better than oneself in order to extract tips from the expert. When two fellow teachers work together each may well act as a mentor on different occasions, even within the same conversation. We make this point to emphasise our view that learning about teaching requires some sort of 'assisted performance'. When Bruner (1977: Preface) wrote about assisted performance for young people, he emphasised that it will 'depend massively upon participation in a dialogue carefully stabilised by the adult partner. So much of learning depends on the need to achieve joint attention, to conduct enterprises jointly, to honour the social relationship between learner and tutor.'

This reference to the 'adult partner' is equally applicable to any teaching relationship. The important point for us here is how the 'carefully stabilised' dialogue can be achieved when the relationship is between colleagues who are not only busy and have a wide range of other commitments, but are also acting on equal terms as both learner and mentor. This emphasises the need for a shared commitment to giving a high priority to improving classroom practice, as well as a shared language to help translate good intentions into positive action. It is for this reason that we have constructed a description of teaching, and a vocabulary for teaching, that we describe below. The next section outlines this description of teaching and how it can be put to use in developing personal competence.

The nine dimensions of teaching

We want to put our ideas in context by looking at an extract from a classroom in which a teacher is working with a class of 6-year olds.

❋ Transcript 2.1

Mrs P:	The first thing I wanted to show you . . . was to remind you about the chart we looked at. We did this one before half term.
	[Mrs P points in turn to each of the fabrics tested]
Mrs P:	We tested the flowery fabric . . . the . . .
Child:	Check.
Mrs P:	Check fabric . . .

Child:	Brown.
Mrs P:	The brown ... the striped ...
Child:	Pattern.
Mrs P:	The pattern – we call it the patterned ... and lastly ...
Child:	Yellow.
Mrs P:	The yellow fabric. That's right. Can anyone remember the tests we gave them? [Silence]
Mrs P:	We did fair tests ... do you remember we did fair tests ... do you remember we had to do a fair test?
Children:	Yes.
Mrs P:	What did we do? [Silence]
Mrs P:	Read what it says. [Points to title] What did we mean when we wrote it?
Jean:	When we did water ...
Mrs P:	The water test, yes ...
Jean:	We did the same with each one ... the same amount [Alex is looking at the person behind him]
Mrs P:	Can you tell us about the burn test, Alex? [Discussion of 'fair tests' of other sorts] ...
Mrs P:	Now when we look at the fabric ... when we did the test we took out [demonstrates] [waits] ... begins with an 'f' but it's not the word 'fabric'
Child:	Oh. Fibre.
Mrs P:	A fibre. Now, today, our test is going to be something different. We haven't got a lot of fabrics ... [Shows a range of different items made from paper to give children a chance to deduce what today's test is about]
Mrs P:	Now. What is the subject of today's science?
Child:	Testing paper with water.
Mrs P:	It looks like testing paper with water. Certainly I've got a lot of paper. I've got different kinds of paper. ...
Mrs P:	How is paper made ... what fibres are used for making paper? Jenny ... Jenny's got something to tell us ... Jenny
Jenny:	I saw people making paper.
Mrs P:	Where?
Jenny:	um ... Wookey Hole.
Mrs P:	In a sort of factory? What were they using?
Jenny:	Can't remember.
Mrs P:	You can't remember what they were using. Now that's the most important thing I think you've forgotten.
Alicia:	I know Wookey Hole.
Mrs P:	You know Wookey Hole. [Turns to a boy at the other side of the group] Tell me again about the poster, Brendan.

Reading this transcript shows that it is typical of a great deal of teaching: teachers tell children things; they hold conversations with them; they monitor what is happening while they are teaching and while children are working; they ask questions and evaluate children's responses, both spoken and written; they develop an appropriate classroom ethos; they organise materials; and so on. What is not so obvious from observing classrooms, but becomes clear during interviews with teachers, is that they are constantly making decisions based on uncertain and incomplete information. They have to play hunches.

The vast amount of decision making that takes place makes it tempting to say that teaching *is* decision making. However, this is unhelpful in two ways. Firstly, it undervalues the enormous amount of knowledge which makes it possible to take those decisions; secondly, it suggests that it is 'decision making' that needs to be practised, again undervaluing how it is that the practice of decision making must relate to real teaching.

There are many ways of describing teaching and Wragg (1994) has summarised both qualitative and quantitative approaches. Teachers can, if they wish, work out their own set of dimensions, criteria, competences or precepts. One such set has been developed by Dunne and Harvard (1992). It is worth looking at this in some detail, not because it is the only way of conceptualising teaching, but rather because it allows one to consider some important aspects of classroom processes. Dunne and Harvard put forward *nine dimensions of teaching* (Figure 2.1):

The nine dimensions of teaching summarise what

Figure 2.1 The nine dimensions of teaching

- *Dimension 0:* ethos
- *Dimension 1:* direct instruction
- *Dimension 2:* management of materials
- *Dimension 3:* guided practice
- *Dimension 4:* structured conversation
- *Dimension 5:* monitoring
- *Dimension 6:* management of order
- *Dimension 7:* planning and preparation
- *Dimension 8:* written evaluation

teachers do in their observable classroom work. It will not be clear simply from reading the list what is meant by each of 'direct instruction', 'guided practice' and so on: we will attend to this later. What might be surprising is that although we have already emphasised how much of the classroom work of teachers involves taking decisions, this does not appear as one of the nine dimensions. There is good reason for this. When teachers take decisions they take them *about something*. They decide whether to pursue a conversation or to end it; they decide whether to intervene by providing an answer or asking a question; and so on. The nine dimensions are the things that teachers take decisions about; taking decisions is the way in which these dimensions are used. We will refer to this again later, after we have expanded further on the dimensions themselves.

Teachers we have worked with have found these nine dimensions a useful, formal way of thinking about classroom work. They are useful when they are thought of, not as a particular lesson consisting of 'direct instruction' or 'structured conversation', but as being the many things that teachers are taking decisions about in every lesson. We can best illustrate this by looking again at Mrs Palmer.

The first part of this transcript shows the teacher rehearsing the names of the various fabrics that were tested. This is an example of dimension 1, direct instruction, since the intention is to instruct the children in the names that were adopted to describe each piece of fabric. This section is shown below:

✳ Transcript 2.2

Mrs P:	The first thing I wanted to show you ... was to remind you about the chart we looked at. We did this one before half term. [Mrs P points in turn to each of the fabrics tested]
Mrs P:	We tested the flowery fabric ... the ...
Child:	Check.
Mrs P:	Check fabric ...
Child:	Brown.
Mrs P:	The brown ... the striped ...
Child:	Pattern.
Mrs P:	The pattern – we call it the patterned ... and lastly ...
Child:	Yellow.
Mrs P:	The yellow fabric. That's right.

The way in which this instructional purpose is

achieved, however, is through dimension 3, guided practice: the child already has some knowledge of the vocabulary that was used previously, but is not likely to provide this in a single utterance unaided, so the teacher provides practice, referring by name to each one in turn.

This same portion of the lesson can be categorised as both direct instruction and guided practice. It will be seen later when each of these dimensions is described in more detail that each focus will add different insights into what is possible in classroom work of this type. For the moment, our purpose is to illustrate roughly what some of the dimensions look like in practice and to confirm that the possibility of more than one interpretation is important in this way of analysing classroom work.

There are other examples of this:

✳ Transcript 2.3

Mrs P:	We did fair tests ... do you remember we did fair tests ... do you remember we had to do a fair test?
Children:	Yes.
Mrs P:	What did we do? [Silence]
Mrs P:	Read what it says. [Points to title] What did we mean when we wrote it?
Jean:	When we did water ...
Mrs P:	The water test, yes ...
Jean:	We did the same with each one ... the same amount. [Alex is looking at the person behind him]
Mrs P:	Can you tell us about the burn test, Alex?

In this extract the teacher is using dimension 4, structured conversation. In general terms, this is a conversation because it involves some sort of dialogue between people (in this case, the teacher and more than one child). It is 'structured' in the sense of being given shape by and having some intention on the part of at least one participant. This is sufficient for us to make the initial categorisation, although the detail of this dimension is more complex. The point here is not the different levels of complexity of the dimension 'structured conversation' but the fact that the last line

Mrs P:	Can you tell us about the burn test, Alex?

can be interpreted as dimension 5, monitoring, because it indicates alertness to what Alex is doing and what he might know, and even to dimension 6, management of order, because it concerns behaviour.

What we have now illustrated is how thinking in the categories of the nine dimensions of teaching can provide a 'handle' for getting to grips with what happens in classrooms. This is useful in itself but we want to go further. At the moment the list of the nine dimensions is only a set of *labels* for aspects of classroom work: we will all have different versions of what they really mean.

We want to establish a clearer definition for each dimension. Although it is possible to do this with a paragraph about each one we have adopted a different approach. We want to use the nine dimensions to aid decision making in classrooms and to provide a route for improving personal competence. For this reason we have described each dimension at a number of levels (seven or eight) ranging from relatively simple levels of performance to more complex expressions of competence. Figure 2.2 shows this for dimension 1, direct instruction, and descriptions of the levels for the full set of nine dimensions is provided in the Appendix.

responses. In order to know whether she is evaluating, and to know how she is making decisions related to the other dimensions, we need to ask her. A short section of a rather lengthy interview with Mrs P is helpful in seeing a teacher make use of the nine dimensions of teaching. Both the interviewer and Mrs P have the written set of dimensions in front of them during the conversation, so they are able to make reference to them.

❇ Transcript 2.4

I: We've had a look at a long piece, a section, of your lesson and talked about several dimensions. Can we, can we look especially, specifically at direct instruction . . .

P: Mm.

I: And look at when Jenny and Alicia mentioned Wookey Hole . . .

P: We've said about Jenny and structured conversation . . . I wasn't able to challenge any points because she did not know . . .

I: Yes. We may return to, . . . have another look at,

Figure 2.2 The criteria for direct instruction

DIMENSION 1: DIRECT INSTRUCTION

1 Attract children's initial interest; maintain appropriate sequence using supplied material for demonstrations and descriptions.

2 For demonstrations and descriptions, organise suitable seating arrangements, introduce material well, use appropriate visual aids, sustain children's interest.

3 Check clarity of explanation by appropriate questions; convey enthusiasm with appropriate verbal and non-verbal behaviour.

4 Choose appropriate examples, analogies and metaphors; explain as well as describe and demonstrate.

5 Choose concepts with both subject matter and children's interests in mind; ensure children's engagement and participation; use a range of examples and aids to meet diversity of children's attainments; summarise key issues.

6 Pace explanation in light of children's responses with regard to interest and comprehension; show grasp of possible content options and justify particular choices.

7 Make explanations efficient and concise; choose examples for their power in the subject.

If we look again at the short episode of Mrs P's teaching it is clear that she is not only using aspects of direct instruction, structured conversation, management of materials and management of order, but is probably also evaluating children's

maybe later. Can we really focus on direct instruction and see how this bit does do that, does some . . .

P: I wanted to give a lesson . . . instruction . . . I was instructing overall in how to make paper . . . so, [reading level 1] 'attract children's initial interest' ... I used the poster of last term's work, when they did various experiments on materials ... I used what they knew from that ...

I: But you did more than use what they know ... look at this bit where you said 'Read what it says ... what did we mean when we wrote that?'

P: Yes, they wouldn't remember it all, but I was making them really use the notes we made last term. Do you see that as a part of creating initial interest?

I: *I* do. It seems a really important example. Do *you?*

P: I hadn't ... but I will use it again ... another bit of work.

I: If we use that as an example of attracting ... if we see this as a good example ... we'll need to work out why this is, to justify ... but keep that for later. Let's trace that bit ... initial interest ... let's look at level 2: sustain children's interest. We may find this in all sorts of places ... what is really interesting is when we find it in unusual places. We're looking at Jenny and Alicia ... and Wookey Hole ... tell me about that again, this time quite specifically in this level 2, direct instruction.

P: So we've said this bit with Jenny is structured conversation and now ...

I: Yes. We could look at the detail of structured conversation, but for the moment let's re-interpret it as direct instruction, let's see what ...

P: OK. So by pausing to ask Jenny about her trip I thought she could tell us about paper-making ...

I: And?

P: And she couldn't, so I moved on.

I: You could have persisted with the conversation.

P: Should I have done?

I: I'm not saying that. We're looking for how we can interpret what you did.

P: The conversation could have been very much about Jenny herself. I might do that, I might do that sometimes. I wanted to talk about making paper ... the others wouldn't have been so involved.

I: And direct instruction?

P: And direct instruction ... sustaining the children's interest – that was more important. I like it.

I: [Laughs] I like it too. But what about Alicia?

P: What about Alicia. I've forgotten.

I: [Points to notes; reads] 'I've been to Wookey Hole', Miss.

P: [Laughs] Alicia's been everywhere. Instinctively I ... what did I say? Instinctively [reads] I said 'Alicia's been to Wookey Hole' and then ... what does this say? Oh yes [reads] ... yes ... I turned back to the poster.

I: Direct instruction?

P: Yes. I could easily have lost the initial interest in the poster ... I knew where I wanted to go. I knew that Alicia's story would be personal – I didn't want that then.

What we see here is how an initial discussion about the fairly obvious occurrence of structured conversation, direct instruction, management of materials and so on is developed by persistent attention to one dimension (and later, but not shown here, equal attention to another dimension). Very detailed discussions like this are especially important for student teachers learning how to teach, as they enable beginners to become clear in their minds about the nature of teaching and how they might progress. Time constraints mean that intensive analysis is generally only possible in those circumstances, that is, when teachers do not have full responsibility for a class and a full teaching timetable. However, aspects of what is described here are also possible for full-time experienced teachers (and this is particularly the case as part of a programmed approach to appraisal). The following activities suggest a way forward.

a ACTIVITY 2

Tape record a small part of your classroom work (about 15 minutes). Transcribe the tape and work out where each of the nine dimensions can be identified (or as many as possible). Select one dimension and work out the relevance of each of the levels to this bit of your classroom work. Do some of the levels suggest alternative courses of action?

a ACTIVITY 3

Observe a colleague for about 15 minutes. Concentrate on just one of the nine dimensions and see how the colleague's work relates to the various levels in that dimension.

If we look again at the transcript of Mrs P's

FEAR + RESPECT = OBEDIENCE

Direct instruction

interview, we can see that both she and the interviewer refer to things that were actually said in the classroom. In our own work with teachers and students we do not usually collect this evidence from audio or video recordings, because they are usually time consuming to do properly, and full transcripts of lessons can run to twenty or thirty pages, which is too detailed to be really useful.

We find it more useful to work from an observer's notes. The usual difficulty with this is that the observer is inevitably biased towards a particular view of classrooms, and such a partial view is not what is needed. A completely impartial view of teaching is simply not possible, as all observers carry their own precepts and perceptions with them. What we want is a version of classroom events that is sensitive to the teacher's intentions, not merely to the observer's bias. One way of doing this is for the teacher and observer to negotiate an agenda, a notion so apparently simple that, until they try it, many people reject it out of hand. We suggest you try it and see for yourself whether it works.

Annotating an agenda during classroom observation

Teachers develop their own ways of writing their plans for a term's work, a week's work and for each lesson. Increasingly, schools are establishing a common format for teachers working in the school. Our approach to preparing a document specifically for use during observation does not interfere with any established or preferred way of recording planning. It is possible to record very valuable information about a colleague's classroom performance in a short episode (15 to 20 minutes) and it is for this sort of episode that we find negotiating and agreeing an *agenda* beforehand is useful.

An agenda is confined to one page of A4 paper, so that people do not become too ambitious; is written on the left-hand side of that page, leaving the right-hand side for the observer's notes; and is a detailed indication of the content and sequence of that short episode, including a note of the dimension to which the observer is asked to attend. For example, an agenda might refer to the introductory remarks at the beginning of a lesson; or a time when the children are working under guidance from the teacher; or the concluding remarks or report-back session; or record a transition between activities.

The detail of the agenda will need to include the crucial things the teacher will say (if possible a guess at the actual words it is intended will be used); and what the teacher will be looking for (e.g. 'if children stuck, show model on side bench'). This is *not* a constraint on what actually happens. If the actual episode is very different from that intended, then this is just as interesting and valid as if everything went as planned. The agenda is written by the teacher who will be teaching the lesson; the observer receives the agenda and uses it for making notes alongside the teacher's written intentions.

There are two interesting aspects in writing an agenda for a short episode:

1   It sounds trivial but usually proves rather difficult to implement.

2   Writing down detailed intentions usually involves extensive revision of them.

@ ACTIVITY 4

1   Write an agenda for two or three different types of short episode (15 to 20 minutes) in lessons you will soon be teaching. Select a dimension for each episode that might focus the observer's attention.

2   Ask a colleague to use the agenda you have written to observe you during an episode and to make notes as objectively as possible about what you said and did, and what the children said and did. Emphasise that it is not intended that everything must be recorded: the observer should make a selection.

3   Sit down with a colleague (possibly the one who observed you, but it could be with someone else) and try to interpret the observer's written notes

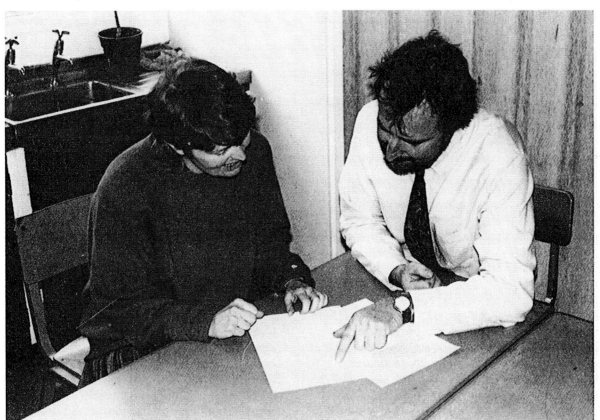

Using an annotated agenda

on the agenda. Start with the dimension that served to focus the observation; then re-interpret the episode by working with a different dimension.

The kind of work described above concentrates on teachers thinking about their own practice and developing it by testing it against the nine dimensions of teaching. This can be very valuable, but what is suggested so far is really a preparation for more deliberately learning from each other. Observers have to beware of the temptation, when watching a lesson, to project some paragon ideal of themselves, or equally to compensate for their own deficiencies. There is a tendency when watching each other teach to do three things:

1 Compare what we see unfavourably with an idealised view of our own teaching.
2 Compare it favourably with our own teaching, asserting that 'I couldn't do it that way', as teaching is very personal.
3 Select a few tips or ideas and then use them in our own way.

The following extended activity is designed specifically to enable two teachers to learn from each other. It needs to be done skilfully and sensitively, as it involves trying out someone else's teaching styles.

a ACTIVITY 5

1 Find a fellow teacher whose class you will be able to teach at some future date by swapping. Observe the colleague teaching her own class during a short, carefully selected episode that has been chosen for its potential usefulness to you. Do not worry at this stage about writing an agenda or even writing notes.
2 On some future occasion take the class yourself for a similar episode. Do this on several occasions if necessary until you feel you are performing in a similar way to what you observed from your colleague. If it is possible for the colleague to observe, on an informal basis, one or more of these episodes and discuss them with you, so much the better.
3 When you feel comfortable with doing that sort of episode, sit down with your colleague and together prepare an agenda for a further, similar piece of teaching. The agenda must include an indication of the dimension that is agreed for the focus of observation.

4 Teach the episode with your colleague formally observing, that is, making notes on the agenda as objectively as possible about what you and the children say and do. The notes will not be a full record of what went on: the observer must make a selection.
5 Set aside a lengthy time (at least an hour, and more if possible) to discuss the agenda with a colleague (on this occasion, preferably *not* the one who observed you). Work together at establishing *what happened* during the episode (from the annotated agenda and your memory); *how this relates* to the various levels in the selected dimension; *how the episode can be re-interpreted* in another dimension.
6 Consider with the people involved in the previous activity:

   a) How your view of the colleague's work changed as you practised the episode.
   b) How your view of the episode changed as you jointly wrote the agenda.
   c) What kind of language you used, and how your view changed, as you discussed the annotated agenda.

The activities described above involved:

- Focusing on a particular aspect of classroom performance.
- Working with a fellow teacher and making sense of that colleague's work.
- Relating performance to the nine dimensions of teaching.

These activities are important because they reveal and practise the decision making that is central to teaching. In most cases, teachers working together to prepare an agenda about an episode which they both *know in a particular sense*, namely, in terms of performance, find that there is a genuine tussle about what the episode is 'really' about. In seeking to achieve some agreement, they make further sense of the purposes and methods within that episode. It would be entirely inappropriate to pay this much attention to every episode that a teacher undertakes: for the sake of sanity, every teacher has to have a considerable range of fairly routine actions. It is in order to improve general effectiveness that we devote so much attention to a small part of the teacher's work. It is the availability of intensive knowledge, and the ability occasionally to draw on it, that is important.

When an observer annotates an agenda, as in the activity above, attention is focused on a particular dimension. Later, when the episode is discussed with another teacher, attention is widened so that any other dimension, or any set of dimensions, can be considered from this one piece of evidence. This wider focus, still based on a quite specific piece of classroom work, brings in many new considerations. Though this emphasises just how complicated teaching is, the extensive analysis by teachers of their own and others' craft knowledge offers a collegial way of improving personal competence.

UNDERSTANDING HOW CHILDREN LEARN

The introduction to Unit 2 referred briefly to the problem of teaching children to read, and that the way teachers act in classrooms is a response to very complex problems. Sometimes it is necessary to adopt a technical vocabulary to analyse teaching in order to improve personal competence. This should be neither obscure nor over-complex, otherwise it will confuse rather than clarify thinking and action. The nine dimensions of teaching described in the previous unit suggested a vocabulary for classroom performance.

In this unit we want to look in some detail at a vocabulary for discussing curriculum. It was indicated in the previous unit that the vocabulary of the National Curriculum is useful but that it is not sufficiently detailed to enable teachers significantly to improve their effectiveness. Looking at the question of reading in particular can introduce a way of thinking and talking about how children learn that is very useful.

This can be illustrated by pretending that there are just three approaches to teaching reading. These three approaches might be, for instance, phonics, look and say, real books. It would be tempting to argue that the teacher's role is to assess each child in order to set him or her on the particular approach that seems suited to the individual. This course of action is summarised in Figure 3.1.

This approach is unsatisfactory. It assumes that children somehow fit schemes: that a scheme accurately reflects how children learn. Most teachers have a high regard for the individuality of children and do not accept that this is the case, so they employ a mixture of methods depending on the context. Figure 3.1 is, therefore, an over-simplification, as teaching is much more complex than that. The reality is that teachers make several successive judgements in which they assess the situation about children's needs, as shown in Figure 3.2, again pretending that there are just three possible approaches.

ACTIVITY 6

Discuss whether Figure 3.1 or Figure 3.2 better summarises your own view of what teaching should be like. Might it be different for different subject areas? What do you in fact do in the classroom?

The idea of diagnosis is, of course, contained in both figures. Figure 3.2 summarises what is often called *formative assessment* and is consistent with the idea

Figure 3.1 An assessment leading to a single approach

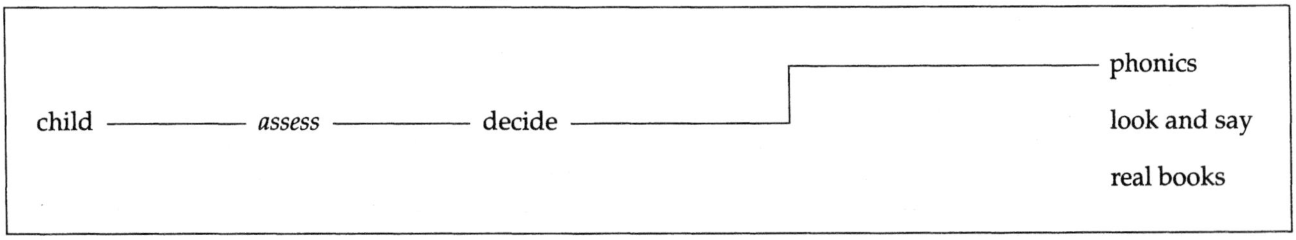

child ——— *assess* ——— decide ——————— phonics

look and say

real books

Figure 3.2   Successive assessments of children's needs

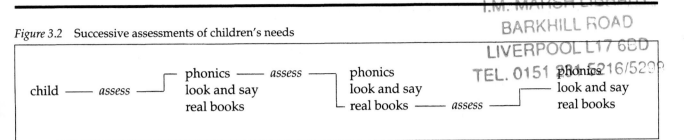

of teachers being continually involved in making decisions based on diagnosis. The notion of 'formative assessment' has become part of the normal vocabulary of teaching since the introduction in 1988 of the National Curriculum and, more specifically, since the publication of the accompanying report on the assessment of children's learning (DES 1988).

The label 'formative assessment' is convenient and it roughly describes something that teachers do, but it omits the real complexity of what takes place. It sounds plausible, but it does not reveal what a messy process it is: how teachers have to struggle with very uncertain information and make difficult decisions, often snap judgements, and modify them and worry about them. This is true not only of 'formative assessment' as a label, but of all labels we use, including for instance 'open-ended questions', 'intelligence' and so on. Labels are sometimes necessary. We put things in categories in order to make sense of the world we live in. That is why we offered the 'nine dimensions of teaching' in Unit 2. The main dangers are that the categories are too broad and losing sight of the problematic nature of them. It is necessary to believe them but not to believe them too much.

A category system for understanding children's learning

Although the Cockcroft Report (DES 1982) dealt with the teaching of mathematics, it made brief mention of a category system that deserves wider usage. Its suggestion in paragraph 241 is one that we have adopted in slightly modified form and developed to be used generally. It is worth considering classroom work as being composed of facts, skills, concepts and strategies. The Cockcroft Report stated that each 'needs separate attention by the teacher' (DES 1982: para. 241). This is a useful set of categories that helps focus thinking about classroom work. It is this system that we discuss below, but first it is worth taking a look at the summary of ideas in Figure 3.3.

Although the terms fact, skill, strategy and concept are quite commonly used there are a number of points that can be usefully made.

Facts

A 'fact' cannot always be worked out logically. For instance, a three-sided figure is called a triangle, but this is only a convention, a choice of word selected and adopted from any number of possibilities. If the word 'triside' or 'threeline' had been selected, then life would have progressed in the same way, with people using the chosen label as confidently as the existing one. It is the common use of the word, because everyone uses it, that makes it 'correct'; there is no intrinsic property of the word that makes it the right one.

It is a convention that a fact must be acquired by the learner and the learner must memorise it. The capital of France is Paris. There is no choice in the matter and it is verifiable in a textbook. Children may be told it or find it out for themselves and then have it confirmed, but one way or another they will need to acquire it as their own. In the case of learning to read, with the vocabulary we are advocating here, the pronunciation of 'ough' in 'bough' is classified as a fact, though there may be regional variations of this 'fact', and all the techniques available for assisting people to memorise things may have to be brought into play when dealing with this.

The idea of a 'fact' and of 'telling' and 'memorising' can be fairly straightforward. There are some aspects of classroom work, however, that can be worked out logically by the child, but teachers may still choose to tell and ask children to memorise. For instance, if children know the words 'two', 'three' and 'five' when linked to the correct number of objects and know something about addition, they could work out that two plus three equals five even if they had not previously met that sum. In this case they would be using some concept of number and of addition to establish something previously unknown. But teachers may decide that 'two plus three equals five' is one of the things that they want children to use in order to understand number and

Figure 3.3 Facts, skills, strategies and concepts

category	What the teacher does	What the child does
fact	tells	memorises
skill	shows	practises
strategy	demonstrates in context	models in context
concept	provides appropriate range of facts, skills, strategies and examples and non-examples of concept	makes connections between facts, skills, strategies based on comparison with examples of concept

addition. In that case they might treat it as a fact and teach it in the same way: by telling and memorising.

Of course, there is an extreme case that will be avoided. It would be bizarre to classify everything as facts and teach only by rote. Teachers have to make conscious decisions about what is to be so nominated as a 'fact to be told', how much children can memorise and what further benefits are to be gained by memorising.

Skills

Skills are relatively straightforward actions, physical or mental, that can be practised in isolation. Cutting along a straight line, drawing an angle with a protractor, adding numbers by using wooden blocks, combining a memorised consonant blend with a memorised vowel sound are all examples of skills. Teaching a skill sometimes requires the teacher to show children how to do it and then provide practice until a certain degree of mastery is achieved. A mental skill, such as 'using one's imagination' or 'solving a problem', is shown to the child by 'talking it through' and practising it often includes the child using the same language.

Strategies

Strategies involve the use of facts or skills, or combinations of them, in context; that is to say, there is a need not only to make use of facts or skills but to select appropriate ones. This is often neglected: relatively little specific teaching attention is given to the demonstration and subsequent modelling of strategies in context. The idea that strategies should be 'demonstrated in context' by the teacher implies a need to talk through how a problem is being tackled, indicating why certain directions are being taken and why others are being discarded. We will emphasise the point later that to do this realistically in a classroom requires that the whole class has some knowledge of a range of facts and skills, so that they can appreciate why they are selected and discarded.

Concepts

The word 'concept' is widely used in education, but is actually rather difficult to define. Information stored as a concept is usable in a wide range of situations including ones very different from those used in the learning process. Someone who can apply the word 'triangle' to, say, each of the four different examples of a triangle actually used by the teacher in teaching it, can apply the label in that context, but may be unable to identify other triangles. Someone who has acquired the concept of 'triangle' will certainly be able to apply it to new examples; more powerful concepts of 'triangle' would allow other information to be brought from the learning context and applied to the new situation. The formation of a concept needs a range of experiences that include associated facts, skills and strategies as well as examples and non-examples of the concept in use.

ACTIVITY 7

1   It is not appropriate to talk about *the* concept of, for instance, a triangle because each of us has our own concept. There must, of course, be a great deal of overlap otherwise we cannot sensibly discuss triangles. Ask each member of the group to draw a triangle without looking at what the others are doing. Then ask each member to draw a second triangle, different in some way from the first one.

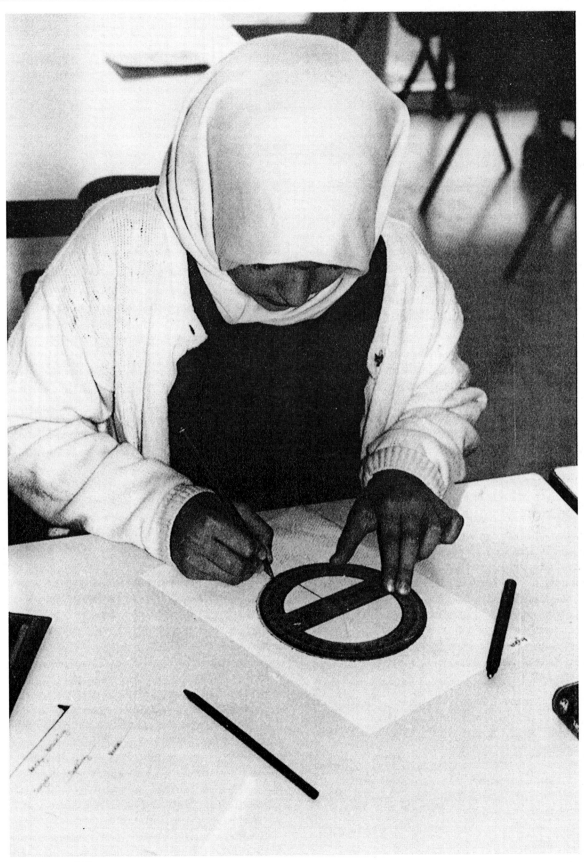

Learning a skill

2 Compare drawings. Did most people draw an equal sided triangle first? Discuss with others what each understands by the word 'triangle'. What range of facts and skills does each associate with teaching children about triangles? Can you draw a triangle on a football?

3 Discuss with others the concept of 'gravity'. How different are members' notions? Consider how 'gravity' might be taught.

One of the other books in this series (Brown and Wragg 1993) discusses the use of questioning in classrooms. A description in that book (p. 11) of a typical sorting and counting exercise in reception classes contains the following remarks about children working with wooden beads painted blue and brown:

> If the pupils are asked 'Are there more brown beads than blue beads?' then most young pupils can answer the question. If the question is posed 'Are there more wooden beads than blue beads?' then some pupils cannot work out the correct answer, others do work out the correct answer and a few think the question is so obvious it is trivial. The pupils who provide the correct answers have managed, in this context, to apply set theory or logic to solve the reasoning problem.

In this present unit we have established a way of describing learning that gives the opportunity to plan teaching strategies that can assist children who are not able to provide a correct answer. This is where the analysis of tasks (Figure 3.3) can help. Let us now consider how this approach can help children sort out the beads.

If we look at the task as it is presented we can identify the following aspects.

- The *facts* associated with this task are the labels: 'beads', 'brown', 'blue', 'wooden'.
- The *skills* are: 'sorting the brown beads'; 'sorting the blue beads', 'counting the blue beads', 'counting the brown beads'.
- The *strategies* are to be exercised in the context of questions starting with 'Are there more . . . ?' and involve (1) comparing the number of brown beads with the number of blue beads; (2) comparing the number of wooden beads with the number of blue beads.

It can be seen from the analysis that there is a lot of emphasis on those beads that are blue and those

that are brown – and a good deal of practice can be given with these, accompanied by specific labelling. The task assumes that the preparatory work with wooden beads has already been done, that children will already know that the beads are 'wooden'. Consequently, the assumption that the children who answer the questions correctly are exhibiting greater overall conceptual knowledge may not be entirely correct. They may merely be more practised at using the label 'wooden' and better able to apply it to beads.

ACTIVITY 8

1 It is not always possible to plan every single topic in fine detail, but it is worthwhile, from time to time, giving extra thought to one particular topic, so that any planning skills thus acquired may subsequently transfer to other topics. Plan a project on 'Energy' for a class of children aged about 9, to run for 4 or 5 weeks. Select what you would nominate as *facts*, *skills*, *strategies* and *concepts* for this topic.

2 How would you find out, either during or at the end of the project, whether children had 'mastered' the necessary *facts*, *skills*, *strategies* and *concepts*?

3 Teach the topic and see how your planning ideas work out in practice. If possible, ask one or more colleagues to do exactly the same exercise and then compare notes and experiences.

This activity raises one of the key ideas associated with facts and skills, namely that of 'mastery'. Although a great deal of work has been done over the years to establish exactly what is meant by this, it has been so difficult to define it clearly that it is not in general use in talk about classrooms. Yet the effective teacher does have clear expectations of what children should achieve and conveys these expectations to the children. One way of expressing this is to discuss and clarify with children before, during and after the project, the level of 'mastery' that is expected. In the terms of the analysis we are using here, this would involve being clear which facts in a topic should be rapidly recalled, what kinds of skill should have been acquired and what are the most important concepts to be understood.

Teachers have to make difficult decisions about which facts will be used sufficiently often to justify emphasising them, and the danger of overloading children must be borne in mind. On the other hand,

Are there more wooden beads than blue beads?

when the level of mastery is carefully specified for certain aspects of the work, children do respond and are further motivated by their success. One example of this is in the early stages of learning to read. Some teachers, whatever general approach they use, select certain words like 'the', 'a', 'an', 'then', 'was' and so on to be treated as facts and memorised for instant recall. In these case, 'mastery' is defined as being able to read the word in context, respond to a flashcard with the word on it and, on hearing the word spoken, to be able to scan a written sentence and locate the word.

'Alright Damian, I think you've mastered it now'

CLASSROOM ORGANISATION AND MANAGEMENT

The framework for discussion

In Unit 2 we suggested a framework for discussing teachers' classroom work. We called this framework the nine dimensions of teaching and used an example from 'direct instruction' quite extensively. This example emphasised how 'attracting initial interest' and 'maintaining interest' is achieved from many different approaches that the teacher might adopt. Many children already begin with a deep interest in a certain topic, but others appear to have less concern and teachers will often have to work hard to arouse interest and then keep it at a high level.

The companion book in this series *Explaining* (Wragg and Brown 1993), gives numerous examples of how teachers seek to attract and then hold children's interest. Sometimes they use an 'advance organiser', what at the beginning of a radio and television programme broadcasters would call a 'tease', a clue that will intrigue and capitalise on curiosity, like asking children to make a guess about something that will come up later in the explanation.

In this unit we will extend the discussion of the same idea of attracting and sustaining interest into questions of classroom organisation and management. We will use this as an example of how important organisation is to the work of the teacher. This discussion could range very widely, and a great deal has been covered in the companion book *Class Management* (Wragg 1993), but the idea here is to illustrate the value of an intensive treatment of particular aspects of organisation and management within the context of the whole school.

We shall focus on one particular aspect of effective teaching, namely the matter of arousing and maintaining pupil interest, by looking at it specifically in the context of organising and

managing a classroom. Let us be a little more specific. The reference to 'interest' in the nine dimensions of teaching described above is contained in the idea of 'direct instruction' (see Figure 2.2 on p. 10), so we need to think how organisation and management can contribute to securing and maintaining children's interest in order to give instruction. The first thing to do is look carefully at what teachers often do in this respect.

Display

Many attractive classrooms have a strong emphasis on display. The use of colour, layout and the mounting of children's work or other educational material, stimulates interest which is maintained by the gradual development of the display through children's involvement in it. There is usually a careful balance between displaying only the finest pieces of work and making sure that each child has something on display that is good by his or her own standards. Some teachers change displays completely at regular intervals and as a matter of principle. Others change parts of the display in sequence, and yet others make judgements about when to change and how much to change.

One teacher made a vivid display of an aspect of the Aztecs with a large amount of pictorial and written information and maintained interest by posing a question twice a week that children could answer by examining the display. To begin with, these questions were written on the board and the teacher specifically drew the children's attention to them; but later they appeared at unpredictable intervals and were placed unobtrusively in the display itself. In this way the teacher ensured that

What are the purposes of display?

the children were constantly searching the display, even to find the questions.

ⓐ ACTIVITY 9

1 Look at the current display in your own or someone else's classroom. What seems to be the purpose of it: To celebrate children's work? To create an attractive environment? Ask yourself about any instructional purpose. What do you, or the teacher whose classroom you are observing, do to sustain interest?
2 Ask other teachers or students to analyse their classroom displays, visiting each other's classrooms wherever possible. Discuss similarities and differences. What can you learn from each other, not only about the purposes, but also about the style of displays and the uses made of them?

Arrangement of furniture

There are numerous reasons for organising the classroom furniture in different ways. In some cases there is an emphasis on enabling the teacher to be vigilant (see Wragg 1993). In other cases there are direct contributions to be made to children's learning as has been discussed in the *Talking and Learning in Groups* (Dunne and Bennett 1990) volume in this series. The question of securing the children's interest does not replace purposes such as these but gives a different focus that enables them to be enhanced. This change in emphasis can be illustrated by recalling how the idea of vigilance was discussed in one respect as 'anticipating problems', where the experienced teacher 'notices that children at one table have finished early and are beginning to distract others' (Wragg 1993: 46).

It may be that this happens in all kinds of classroom work including, for instance, during cooperative group work. Sometimes these kinds of group are organised as 'working individually on identical tasks for individual products' (Dunne and Bennett 1990: 16). If teachers can focus on the notion of 'maintaining interest', then this provides another way of thinking about this problem.

One teacher, when she analysed her own work in the light of how best to maintain children's interest in what they were doing, concluded that she was too often put in the position that she had to talk right across the whole classroom to deal with some situation, so she decided to reorganise the furniture to help in solving the problem. She had already tried ensuring that each piece of work she provided should include a more extending and problematic element at the end, that would really make children think hard, but found that this was not sufficient.

Next she reflected on her practice of writing a series of instructions for different groups on the board near her desk, as this was in some sense too 'distant' for maintaining interest. She experimented with individual sheets for each child but found these costly and inconvenient to prepare as well as untidy in the classroom. She produced a sheet for each group backed with card but found that the passing of these among the group was in itself a problem.

After several such experiments she finally tried a rearrangement of furniture. Her pursuit of 'maintaining interest' involved moving away from her customary practice of grouping children around all sides of a table. Instead she rearranged the tables so that one side of each group's table was butted against a wall. This allowed her to use the wall for pinning task details for each group. It was not necessarily the solution that another teacher might have devised, nor would it have always been possible in another type of classroom, but it illustrates how it is possible for any teacher to consider various possibilities and come up with a solution that she judges to be the most effective for her particular circumstances.

a ACTIVITY 10

1 Look at the arrangement of furniture in your own or another teacher's classroom and consider how best the arrangement of furniture might meet the instructional purpose of achieving and maintaining interest.
2 Visit other classrooms and invite other teachers to your own room. Discuss how each teacher might arrange furniture to maximise opportunities for arousing and maintaining pupil interest.

Rules

The idea of analysing classroom rules in terms of the instructional function of achieving and maintaining children's interest is initially puzzling. When we have worked with teachers on this aspect, to begin with it has seemed a curious idea to them. However, there is a great deal to be gained from taking this approach as can be seen from a brief look at some ways in which experienced teachers intuitively approach this. The question of classroom rules is covered in the companion book in this series on *Class Management* (Wragg 1993).

Some teachers give rules to their new pupils, others adopt the idea of negotiating rules with their classes. There is often a debate among teachers as to the extent to which this is 'genuine negotiation' and to what extent it is a subtle way of imposing rules on children. What is interesting about seeing this process and its results in many classrooms is the uniformity of the rules that are generated, and we found in the Leverhulme Primary Project that the most common rules dealt with talking, movement and children's work. Rules such as 'No talking when the teacher (or someone else) is talking' were commonplace.

Analysis of negotiated rule setting from the perspective of 'arousing and maintaining interest' raises the question not of whether genuine or sham negotiation takes place, but the extent to which it is successful as an instructional process. One teacher we interviewed commented: 'If they've come up with the ideas themselves ... if it's their own ... then you can say, well, why are you doing that? It was your idea to have that, you agreed to that rule. There's a kind of pressure.' Another teacher suggested: 'It's not a question of using the rules as a lever ... a kind of moral blackmail ... it's more to do with understanding the rules. It's like any bit of teaching really ... discussion is necessary.'

A student teacher who pursued the idea of 'maintaining interest' through the use of negotiated rules came up with an unusual approach. She made her set of rules, which were displayed in the classroom, the centre of continuing interest by asking pairs of children in turn, throughout the term, to collect and report examples of the rules being observed by the class. She made time to discuss the report with the authors before it became public and removed the specific instances of misbehaviour (there was a tendency at first to want to report wrong-doers), so that children could concentrate on the general matter of rule observation.

Is the furniture in the best place?

ACTIVITY 11

1　Consider the extent to which negotiated rules are utilised in your own or someone else's classroom. How do you and the children view the instructional purpose of negotiation?

2　Discuss classroom rules with fellow teachers or students in the light of the requirement to 'arouse and maintain children's interest in their work'.

Teaching style

Primary teachers employ a range of approaches to teaching that can be summarised as the use of individual work, group work and class teaching. The first activity in the accompanying volume *Talking and Learning in Groups* (Dunne and Bennett 1990) invites readers to assess the extent to which they use each of these forms of organisation. Sometimes teachers adopt a particular style of teaching almost to the exclusion of others; sometimes a range of styles is employed for different purposes. Reasons given for each of these will vary, sometimes referring to the need for children to experience variety, sometimes referring to the teacher's own preference and on other occasions pointing to the requirements of different types of work.

Given our focus at the moment on 'achieving and maintaining interest', it seems that the notion of 'variety' is immediately relevant. That is certainly the case, but it is also possible to look beyond the single idea of a 'need for variety'. If we continue to emphasise a concern for 'interest' related to an instructional purpose, then a perceived need for variety must be related to learning. But under what conditions does variety assist learning?

Certainly, each of the different aspects of learning described in Unit 3 demands a different treatment, and this is important. The question remains, however, is variety in itself useful? This is difficult to answer, as there is no conclusive research evidence. Indeed, there are different interpretations of what 'variety' actually means, whether it is changing the stimulus, the style adopted by the teacher, the pupils' activities or what. This means that it is more fruitful to look at what kinds of variety children actually experience, than hope there are universal prescriptions that fit any circumstance.

Analysing one's own teaching and making notes about what variety seems to occur, for example in terms of the teaching styles used, the activities children engage in, the construction of some of their lessons, is well worthwhile. So is observing other teachers and encouraging a colleague to watch you. As part of a whole-school policy for improving effectiveness, many questions can be raised. Notes can be compared between teachers to see what range of styles a child moving from one year group to another, as they are currently staffed, would experience over, say, three years. Is there a variety of style? If you think this is useful in sustaining interest in learning, should there be a greater variety in one year? Does each teacher provide the same range as a group of teachers? Are individual teachers particularly effective using one style rather than another?

Assessment

Assessment of one sort or another features in primary classrooms rather more significantly than in recent years. There remains a concern among many that assessment tends to distort the educational process unless it is done without the children knowing it is going on. There is a real concern that on the one hand children will under-perform through nervousness, and on the other hand that they will work only for the test to the exclusion of those things that cannot readily be tested. Arguments for and against such points of view must always rest to a great extent on assertion and counter-assertion rather than on hard evidence.

A major difficulty is that the type of test, the purposes of the test and the context in which tests are taken are all crucial to this debate. Our approach here is to look at the question from another perspective. Given that tests *are* used in classrooms, how can we ensure that they are employed in the pursuit of instruction and that children actually learn better as a result? In particular, how can we use tests to maintain interest in those things that we judge to be worthwhile? This question will be further addressed in Unit 6.

Monitoring pupils' work

In order for teachers to be able to awaken and maintain children's interest, pupils need to behave in a positive way. Again it is worth looking at the management of children's behaviour from this same perspective. Dimension 6 of the nine dimensions of teaching discussed in Unit 2 is about the management of order, and we have already mentioned some elements of this in the section above on classroom rules. However, it is worth considering in this context the important matter of monitoring pupils' work.

Sometimes teachers are disappointed in how little pupils appear to have done by the end of a lesson. Those who monitor work regularly are less surprised. The question is, can monitoring be used not just to check up on progress but also to arouse and maintain children's interest?

a ACTIVITY 12

Consider the eight levels of dimension 5 of the nine dimensions. They are as follows:

Dimension 5: Monitoring

1 Observe children working and intervene to sustain the momentum of the work.
2 Check children can follow and complete the work set.
3 Monitor in order to sustain order and momentum of work; give appropriate feedback; keep simple records of evaluation.
4 Monitor flow of work to sustain availability of resources and ensure efficient transitions; monitor use of time; detect problems of order early; keep thorough records of attainment.
5 Explore children's understanding of work set; make appropriate observations and attempt hunches to explain children's responses; keep records of evaluation.
6 Use monitoring to create hypotheses about children's difficulties; attempt to analyse and test hunches; use monitoring to inform larger-scale adjustments of teaching.
7 Create time for and attempt deeper diagnosis of children's responses to tasks.
8 Sustain a broad programme of diagnostic teaching.

Ask yourself what you understand by each of these levels. Consider how each might involve securing and enhancing children's interest in the topic concerned and try to think of or look out for examples of something that happens in the classroom to illustrate any observation you might have. See if you can come up with a better formulation than dimension 5 above of the nature of monitoring and its impact on children's interest.

Monitoring pupils' work

INSTRUCTIONAL DESIGN

The idea of instructional design

A teacher's classroom performance is one aspect of professional work. In the units above we introduced a range of approaches that can help fellow teachers share and use a particular vocabulary to enhance classroom performance within the whole school. We emphasised how a central element in teaching is the decision making that is constantly necessary to respond to and capitalise on changing circumstances. This involves making decisions about which classroom skills to employ and in what way to use them. But teaching involves decision making that goes beyond the selection of the appropriate teaching skills.

It is now quite common for teachers to be observed at work in the classroom. Some of the many approaches to classroom observation are described in the book *An Introduction to Classroom Observation*, also published by Routledge (Wragg 1994). Classroom assistants, fellow teachers, headteachers, inspectors and occasionally governors, all see teachers at work for a range of different reasons.

It is interesting to reflect that only certain aspects of what teachers do are observable and that little of what is observable is normally noticed. Of course, some observers are very sophisticated and see more than others (and the use of the nine dimensions of teaching can be helpful) but all observers tend to concentrate on relatively superficial features. It is certainly the case that training is needed for classroom observation. However, what interests us here is not those features that are missed by the observer, nor those things that are seen but misinterpreted. We are interested in those things that cannot be seen. The invisible features are the decisions which teachers make.

We are going to concentrate in this unit on how teaching can become more effective when attention is focused on how decisions are made. Again, as when introducing the shared vocabulary of the nine dimensions of teaching, we put emphasis on a common language. As a result of what teachers do in their classrooms, children will listen, write, speak and so on. These observable aspects of what the teacher and children appear to do in the classroom are often cited as examples of 'teaching' and it is this that is central to the work of the teacher.

Although what is observed is central, it is still only a small part of what the teacher is actually doing. Many other aspects are invisible to the observer but are crucially important. It is these other aspects that need exploring, together with how they constitute what we shall call the teacher's 'instructional design'. This term is used to summarise the complex process in which teachers are involved when they provide an example of teaching. We begin by showing in diagrammatic form how an example of teaching is related to the teacher's overall instructional design.

It can be seen from Figure 5.1 that we are suggesting that any example of teaching, the central, observable part of classroom life, is based on six elements. Each of these is described below.

An understanding of how children learn

There is no clearly defined set of readings that constitutes the psychology curriculum for the initial or further training of teachers, so different people have substantially different backgrounds in their knowledge about how children learn. Even when the writings of Piaget were sufficiently popular to be included in almost every course of training, there was no consistent view of their relevance to classroom teaching. Sometimes, knowledge from psychology that was incorporated uncritically into the educational world has been later discredited.

Work in the psychology of learning has brought forward ideas that can be examined for their relevance to classrooms and aspects are included in

Figure 5.1   A model of instructional design using the nine dimensions of teaching

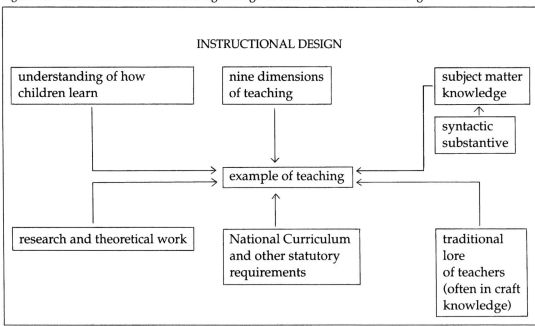

current training courses, as with the work of Bruner and Vygotsky, which may be unknown to established teachers, yet quite familiar to those more recently qualified. Of course, not all that is known about children's learning is derived from the work of psychologists: teachers gain a great deal of knowledge from their own observations, both in classrooms and of other children. What is clear is that there is a wide range of ideas available about how children learn.

The important point about this range of knowledge of children's learning, whether it originally derived from textbook study or personal insight and experience, is that it comprises a vast reservoir of knowledge in every school about how children learn. The question is how to tap this reservoir. There is a great deal of interest and value to be gained from every teacher reading widely about the nature of learning, but teachers also have to read widely about the subject matter they teach, so time constraints must be taken into account. The emphasis we constantly put on working deliberately and analytically with fellow teachers is based on the premise that it is knowledge in use that is most appropriate to engage with: knowledge that is immediately relevant to professional life. Teaching would be the poorer without *any* new knowledge, but the major part of on-going, universal staff development has this different priority.

The nine dimensions of teaching

There are many ways of describing classroom teaching. The nine dimensions of teaching, described more fully in Unit 2 and given in full in the Appendix, have the particular quality of characterising each dimension as a progression from relatively simple levels of performance to more complex expressions of competence. This particular approach, trying to move systematically to higher levels of competence which are explicit and can be consulted by anyone, will not necessarily be already known to teachers.

Even so, a teacher's instructional design will always include some reference to what is possible and desirable in the performance parts of the example of teaching. This particular set of nine dimensions provides a vocabulary that allows more specific description and analysis of what happens in the classroom. It is perfectly possible for anyone who does not agree with this particular formulation to construct a different one of their own making.

Subject-matter knowledge

Subject-matter knowledge for primary teaching presents a considerable problem: the most popular way of organising primary schools with general class teachers taking all, or nearly all, subjects is extremely demanding. This problem will be addressed once more in Unit 6. Whatever form of school organisation is adopted and whether or not the demands are too great, there are some important features of subject-matter knowledge which impinge on instructional design:

1 The National Curriculum does not offer a sufficiently complete description for instructional design for the subject matter it refers to.
2 Published materials cannot in themselves comprise an instructional design for teaching.
3 Instructional design must draw upon some knowledge of the important key concepts of a subject (the substantive knowledge of the subject).
4 Instructional design must draw on some knowledge of the ways of working in a subject, that is, what practitioners actually do (the syntactic knowledge of a subject).

Research and theoretical work

Educational research and the theoretical work that goes with it has in the past often been consigned to the attic after initial training is completed. Nowadays many teachers are involved in researching and producing ideas while studying for advanced qualifications, like the M.Ed. degree and other INSET activities. The effect of these courses on personal practice is often immense, but it is difficult for an individual teacher or head who happens to be enthusiastically working towards further qualifications to achieve a school-wide adoption of ideas or to sustain the thrust alone.

It is all too easy to become frustrated and to dream of a time when all teachers would continually be involved in research, energetically seeking and applying new knowledge. It is more realistic, however, to aim for creating a dynamic school in which the conditions are created for the teachers' knowledge to be implemented by colleagues. It is for this reason that the matter of research and theoretical considerations are included in the instructional design. One major advantage of collaborative activity is the possibility it offers of genuine critique of knowledge in practice: its usefulness can be examined in the context of specific schools. In the truly dynamic school teachers can use theoretical knowledge as appropriate, and avoid the *uncritical* adoption of new ideas.

The accompanying books in this series offer both theoretical and practical support for this kind of reflection and action. In using the books on questioning and explaining by Wragg and Brown, or the book on group work by Dunne and Bennett as INSET materials, each teacher can utilise different ideas. The conscious placing of these ideas into individual teachers' instructional design

should enable these to be examined collaboratively as well.

The National Curriculum and other statutory requirements

The National Curriculum is a legally prescribed requirement. However, it is refined, interpreted and developed in each individual school, so that its various demands are seen not as a prescription for teaching but as a guide. It is clearly part of the instructional design of every teacher, but needs treating in the same way as each of the other aspects.

Indeed it is a considerable challenge to incorporate the requirements of the National Curriculum into one's own instructional design, and it offers yet another opportunity for teachers to compare practice. It is well worth considering how each teacher in a school interprets and incorporates the National Curriculum, what differences and similarities there are, and whether there is a logical, smooth and coherent progression from the children's point of view, or merely a set of disjointed experiences.

The traditional lore of teachers

There is no textbook that can provide the sort of knowledge that teachers develop and store from their daily contact with classes. A lot of it will be specific to a school because of the layout of the buildings or the idiosyncrasies of the current headteacher, pupils, fellow teachers or others engaged in the school's affairs.

Some of it applies more widely, and might refer to how long to spend on particular types of work, how to deal with a marauding wasp or twenty rulers and rubbers, how to vary the demands of an activity mid-stream, or how to spot a distraction before it happens. Some of it is translated into tips for students, the most common being 'start strictly, you can always ease off later', or 'make sure you learn pupils' names quickly'. Though sometimes deprecated for being superficial and atheoretical, teachers' lore does have a place in the improvement of teaching. First of all it does exist, whether everyone subscribes to it or not; secondly, it may contain valuable and relevant distilled wisdom that could be useful to others; thirdly, it may be wrong and need some critical scrutiny.

a ACTIVITY 13

Look at Figure 5.1 on p. 30. Select an example of teaching from your recent classroom work. The example of teaching can be of any length, but for this activity it is best to choose a fairly short episode. Remember that the idea of an example of teaching is that it includes not only what you intended and did, but also what the children did. Now reflect on each of the other boxes in the diagram, trying to decide what you drew on consciously, or might have drawn on without fully realising it during this episode. For example:

- What was the place of subject knowledge?
- Were you caught out by children's questions?
- Were there instances where you reacted to a child in a certain way because of what you knew about his or her ability to learn?
- How did the National Curriculum figure?
- Did anything happen that enhanced, however modestly, your understanding of a particular child, event, or teaching strategy?
- Did any of the nine dimensions used in this book seem particularly relevant, like the management of order or materials, preparation and planning, or a conversation with an individual or group?
- On the basis of what happened, what tip might you give to a fellow teacher or student about practice in the classroom? What would be the basis for such a tip?

The seven aspects highlighted here are, of course, just a part of the story. It is quite possible to be an expert, on the surface at least, in each of these, yet still not be effective as a teacher. The most important part of the story lies in the lines that join these seven aspects to the 'example of teaching'. These lines imply not only that each aspect may contribute to the overall design, but also that complex and delicate judgements have to be made about what weight must be given to each. It is these judgements and the consequent decision making about the seven aspects that can be described as the pedagogical knowledge of teaching.

Pedagogical knowledge

Activity 13 actually concentrated on the pedagogical knowledge of teaching: the detailed decision making that draws on so many aspects of teachers' knowledge. Described in this way, pedagogical knowledge is not easily observable, nor can it always be written down. The various constituent parts can be described to some extent, but are different for different teachers. There is no guarantee that any particular collection of knowledge is either necessary or sufficient for effective teaching.

This does not mean that teachers are unable to enhance their effectiveness. What is needed is that from time to time teachers examine with their colleagues how they make pedagogical decisions and how these might differ if different aspects were emphasised. In other words, Activity 13, like many of the other activities described in this book and the companion volumes, offers something that could usefully feature in a staff development or appraisal programme.

Two points must be emphasised about this sort of activity. Firstly, it must be occasional (and that is why we suggest it as part of a formal staff review), or we would spend our entire life agonising about what is possible at the expense of getting on with the job. Secondly, in order to become a significant part of a dynamic school, this process must be given sufficient time and preparation, otherwise it is likely to remain superficial – a rather comfortable affirmation of current practice.

The key to enhancing effectiveness is in working with professional colleagues with a sufficient degree of formality to allow genuine challenge. This challenge is not merely to argue and defend one's corner, nor a generalised determination to 'make you think', but to allow practitioners scope for considering rationally and collaboratively workable alternatives relevant to their task in a manner that makes it possible to incorporate new ideas. That is the nature of the truly dynamic school. It creates an environment where open discussion of practice is an ordinary rather than extraordinary affair and where teachers are not afraid to examine their own and their colleagues' practice so that all can improve the effectiveness of what they do. In the final unit of this book we shall explore how that positive whole-school approach might be taken further.

WHOLE-SCHOOL ISSUES

In this book we have tried to describe not only how individual teachers can become more effective, but also how a whole-school staff, head and teachers, can work together to amplify what each might do alone. In the dynamic school the judicious management of change for the better is central on the agenda. This does not mean following every fad and fashion, however silly, but rather being constantly on the alert, weighing up and analysing what is taking place, and then initiating major or minor changes in the light of considered evidence, for no school can stand still.

There are many ways in which this can be done. They include the following:

- Individual teachers analysing in detail, from time to time, aspects of their teaching.
- Staff meetings considering specific elements of teaching and learning, such as the use of topic and project work, different ways of explaining, children with learning difficulties, very able pupils, group work, class management, and several others.
- Some systematic monitoring of what takes place, such as teachers watching each other perform with a particular focus on a topic of mutual concern.
- Someone taking the lead, the head or a teacher, to run a seminar on a matter of common interest.
- Studying videos of classroom events to discuss principles and practice.
- Establishing a small task force or working party to explore ways of improving some aspects of the school's work.

The books in this series offer numerous ideas for activities, workshops and ways of observing and analysing teaching and learning, but without determination and drive from all teachers in a school, nothing of note can happen. Schools do not become dynamic by accident, they do so because the people in them take steps to ensure that improving effectiveness is high on the agenda.

Changes in practice are mostly gradual, with teachers taking stock occasionally and fine tuning what they do. If this were not the case, then most practitioners would be submerged under constant change and not be able to do their job properly. Sometimes it is worthwhile contemplating the possibility of a radical look at what is happening in classrooms and in the school, not on a regular basis, as there are limits to what can be done and changes should in any case be given a few years to run, rather than be renegotiated every five minutes, but perhaps every few years.

Radical change should not be considered just to shake people up. It is important to come at issues from a fresh angle occasionally so that what is taken for granted can be discussed rationally and in a positive climate, without threat or blame. We conclude this unit and this book with a special look at a matter of general concern, the issue of how best to individualise learning for children. This lies at the heart of effective teaching, for teachers need to teach the whole class or small groups skilfully, and then there are always times when children are set individual tasks or when the teacher works with a single child, trying to tailor what is done to the individual.

The appropriateness of the task, the teacher's ability to match the work to the individual pupil, to differentiate and know when to provide extension work or to consolidate, are all matters which figure prominently in reports on teaching or on effectiveness generally. We conclude, therefore, by posing a challenge: how can teachers maximise the quality of their work with individual pupils and with the whole class? This may involve reviewing cherished practices and ways of working. We offer one way of considering this, while stressing that there are many others. The exercise below allows a group of teachers in a school to look at alternative frameworks for what they do. The intention is not to offer a single model, but rather to provide a structure for discussion and debate.

The focus on individualisation

Anyone who spends time with groups of children cannot help but notice how different they are from each other and how difficult it is to cater for each of them. The physical differences are fairly obvious, but differences in personality, ability, learning styles and personal preferences are also important. This is often discussed at clinics, playgroups and when parents compare their own children with others. Teachers are usually very clear about these differences as they are faced day by day with the equally startling differences in what children know and can do and how rapidly they learn. It is not surprising that these individual differences have become a major focus for the professional concern of teachers.

There has been considerable encouragement for this emphasis. The Plowden Report (CACE, 1967) made the claim that:

 We found that the Hadow reports understated rather than over estimated the differences between children. They are too great for the children to be tidily assigned to streams or types of schools. Children are unequal in their endowment and in their rates of development .... We conclude that the Hadow emphasis on the individual was right though we would wish to take it further. Whatever form of organisation is adopted, teachers will have to adapt their methods to individuals within a class or school. Only in this way can the needs of gifted and slow children and all those between the extremes can be met.

(p. 460, para. 1232)

This view found further support in the Bullock Report (DES, 1975) which called for 'Careful organisation ... in the planning for each individual child as well as for the class as a whole' (p. 523, para. 85) and asserted that 'individual attention should not be confined to poor readers' (p. 524, para. 86).

These and similar assertions seem to have been influential in consolidating the view summarised in the Cockcroft Report (DES, 1982) that teachers

 must take into account the great variation which exists between pupils both in their rate of learning and also in their level of attainment at any given age. It follows that mathematics courses must be matched both in their level and pace to the needs of pupils; and therefore that a 'differentiated curriculum' must be provided so that pupils will be enabled to develop to the full their mathematical skill and understanding.

(p. 243, para. 801)

It is in these words from the Cockcroft Report that we see most clearly what is common in the other reports: that the differences in children are taken to imply unproblematically that the curriculum must be differentiated; and so insistent is this demand that the need for differentiation has become one of the guiding principles in planning classroom work. The argument that is offered is simply this: 'The obvious fact that children are different from each other implies they must have different treatment.' Is this true? Well, not necessarily. We want to view the statement 'children should be given different treatment' as a genuine problem rather than assume that it is the ultimate aim of education.

A theory of learning

The aspiration to individualise often founders on the realities of working with large groups. A one-to-one relationship in teaching is often assumed to be the ideal in all situations; and it is then assumed that teaching a whole class is a poor substitute for teaching that ideally should be to individuals. What this leads to is teachers trying to emulate individual teaching in the face of impossible management problems. This can be a recipe for failure, ensuring that teachers have to live with a continuing sense of guilt and a sense of unease when they are observed or inspected, sometimes against criteria that are not only impossible to achieve, but are also in some cases inappropriate.

If children were educated alone, and this is not unknown at points in history and among some social groups, then we would have to provide a curriculum that was based on an analysis of their specific needs. But in schools children are in practice educated in larger groups, and a group is not only a collection of individuals. It is in the ways that a group differs from a collection of individuals that holds the key to why an over-emphasis on differentiation may be wrong. The design of the curriculum for educating children in schools must take into account the realities of schools. In recognising this, we need to consider not only the many ways in which children are different from each other but how they are similar; and how we can emphasise and respond to those things, relevant to learning, that are rather similar.

Children are different from each other physically, temperamentally, in what they know, and there are similarly large differences in the way they learn. This suggestion is supported by much of what we can observe about children learning. This has led to an assertion that has become so popular in educational literature that it seems almost an impertinence to challenge it. Ausubel (1968) offered the opinion that: 'If I had to reduce all of educational psychology to just one principle I would say this: the most important single factor influencing learning is what the learner already knows. Ascertain this and teach him accordingly.' This quotation correctly points to the primacy in learning of prior knowledge ('what the learner already knows'); it mistakenly converts this to an assertion about teaching ('teach him accordingly').

Taken to an extreme this commonly held view would condemn the teacher to an ever more complex set of individual assignments, or a sense of failure. Sometimes popular assumptions need turning on their head. An alternative view is that the teacher should not always to seek to respond to every individual difference in children; but that in relation to certain intended outcomes in classroom work, the teacher should attempt to reduce the differences in children.

There are classrooms where learning is individualised, but in which the teacher also works beyond this to provide for higher-order questioning and class discussion based on previous work. It is too easy to emphasise only the individualised aspects without appreciating the particular conditions that make it effective. It is worth discussing how school organisation, not just classroom organisation, can contribute to the management of learning; and we want to look closely at the design of the several parts of the programme.

There has been some attempt (Alexander *et al.*, 1993) to redress the balance of emphasis, arguing that it is the difficulty of managing complex classroom organisation that provides the rationale for whole-class teaching, but the danger is that a climate is created in schools in which class teaching is adopted for its own sake. This is not a sufficient rationale for changes in practice: introducing more class teaching will not in itself solve problems of learning and motivation. In fact, the management of instruction of large groups can be more difficult than approaches that emphasise individuality.

The problems of teaching whole classes are well known. These include the difficulty of providing material, even the spoken word, that can be understood by everyone, yet is sufficiently demanding for the most accomplished. It was teachers' frustration and concern about this that prompted the adoption of individual work and group work. In the Leverhulme Primary Project we found in our studies of experienced primary teachers at work that the split between whole-class teaching and individual or group work was roughly one-third of the former and two-thirds of the latter.

Any shift in balance towards more whole-class teaching needs careful planning and forethought, in full recognition of its intended purposes. There can be advantages to be gained from sessions with large groups, even larger perhaps than the 'normal' class, so long as these are put in place for the following reasons:

1 The work done by children in these sessions is that which is possible and can best be done in a large group.
2 The economy of scale afforded by large groups is then translated into the provision of small group sessions.
3 The work subsequently done by children in small group sessions is that which makes full use of this numerical advantage.

Organising the curriculum

Intelligent planning is needed to organise and teach a school's curriculum in such a way that the best is derived for both large- and small-group work. The form of organisation of the curriculum might mean not only cutting across subject boundaries, but also cutting across the different boundaries typically put in place by 'topic work' or 'projects'. It may also mean some structural changes to school buildings, though imaginative rethinking and flexible use of space are possible in existing buildings. An individual analysis in each school is necessary, recognising the many different circumstances in which teaching and learning take place. When radical change is contemplated, a school's organisational policy is crucial. It is not usually possible for individual teachers to try big changes in isolation.

We describe below how greater effectiveness in teaching can be attempted by exploring a new form of organisation. The extent to which this is possible and desirable will depend on matters peculiar to one's own school, including the number of children on roll, the size of classrooms, the architecture, and so on. In order to flesh out the discussion we provide some statistics for one school. This is done only by way of illustration.

An illustrative example – Newtown Primary School

205 children

11 full-time teachers + headteacher + part-time teachers as follows:
0.3 = special needs, 0.3 = music, 0.1 = classroom release for headteacher

+ one full-time assistant + several part-time assistants

Eight classes:

Three infant age (5- to 7-year-old) classes, with 77 pupils, and five junior age (7- to 11-year-old) classes with 128 children

The school has places for up to 210 children and has eight classrooms.

The school statistics above are representative of a medium-sized primary school. We want to use this as an example to explore some ideas about school organisation. The school has eight classes. Let us first abandon the idea that this means that each of eight groups of children remains together for all teaching and learning activities. We will retain the idea that each child belongs to a group of about thirty children, closely associated with a member of staff, offering security and a base for their work. Let us call this a *base group*. But we want to explore the organisational possibilities by being open-minded about class sizes, attention span and methods of working. There are 128 children, aged 7 to 11 distributed across 4 year groups. Figure 6.1 shows a possible timetable for one day for this group.

It can be seen from Figure 6.1 that during session 1 and session 3 the Y3 and Y4 children (64 of them) are working with one teacher, and in the other two sessions the Y5 and Y6 children are working with one teacher. If we look at session 1, the fact that one teacher takes all the Y3 and Y4 children allows small-group sessions with the Y5 and Y6 children because four teachers are available. There would be very little advantage from this kind of deployment of staff, and indeed many difficulties, if the work in these different large- and small-group sessions were similar. The whole point of this organisation is that the large-group session (lg) involves work that is clearly suited to and planned for such a group. It would not be in a single subject area for the whole session, it would need a skilful teacher to handle it, and it would be inappropriate to select work that would be more suited to small group discussion or complex materials. Similarly, and equally importantly, it would be wrong to squander the resources, especially the teachers' time, in the small-group session (sg), on work that does not need that kind of close contact.

In order to ensure that appropriate work is undertaken in each session and that the sessions are appropriately related there is a need for very detailed planning. How will this be achieved? Here again we want to challenge some assumptions. It is usually assumed that a team working together on a teaching programme needs to plan it jointly in order to incorporate disparate points of view and to achieve joint 'ownership' of the programme.

A structure of the kind suggested above requires a well focused thrust on learning to achieve consistency and best use of time and space, as well as a commitment on the part of the whole team to adopt and implement something that might lead to

Figure 6.1   Day's timetable for 7- to 11-year olds, showing group size and staffing

09.00	09.30	10.00	10.30	11.00	11.30	12.00	12.30	13.00	13.30	14.00	14.30	15.00
Base group	Y3 + Y4: lg (64ch+1t)		*Base group + break*	Y3 + Y4: sg (64ch + 4t)			*Break*		Y3 + Y4: lg (64ch + 1t)		Y3 + Y4: sg (64 ch + 4t)	
	Y5 + Y6:sg (64ch + 4t)			Y5 + Y6: lg (64ch + 1t)					Y5 + Y6: sg (64ch + 4t)		Y5 + Y6: lg (64ch + 1t)	
	session 1			*session 2*					*session 3*		*session 4*	

Notes

lg = large-group session   sg = small-group session   ch = children   t = teachers   Y3 = 7- to 8-year olds   Y4 = 8- to 9-year olds
Y5 = 9- to 10-year olds   Y6 = 10- to 11-year olds

more effective teaching. It needs a deliberate approach to evaluation, and detailed attention to understanding the intended purpose of any change and of each type of activity, rather than a too easy rejection of the model because it is not the same as the present timetable and organisation structure.

It is not our purpose at the moment to attend to the matter of planning work within this structure. It is worth pointing out, however, that other adults, including, if available, part-time staff, ancillaries, parent helpers and student teachers, can be used very effectively in this arrangement. For the moment the younger 5- to 7-year-old children are not included. The proposed organisation for the 7- to 11-year olds provides for the large-group sessions to be complemented by an equal time of small-group sessions. The daunting looking staff–pupil ratio of 1:64 for large-group work enables small groups of 16 to take place. Carefully planned work can make both large and small groups productive: the large-group session, handled well, is not something to be regretted.

But to return to the organisational question: if we decide to include the 5- to 7-year-old children in a similar arrangement, we have to solve the problem of not having enough of them to allow the economy of scale utilised in Figure 6.1. We might choose to solve this by abandoning the infant and junior division at age 7, and go for a half and half split, with 3-year groups, 5 to 8, in one cohort and 3-year groups, 8 to 11, in a second older cohort.

@ ACTIVITY 14

1 Look at the organisation described above (with an open mind!). Assume that you want to organise your school timetable with half the time available for large-group sessions and half the time on small-group sessions. Consider organisational and physical details, e.g. the number of children, the size of rooms and the suitability of furniture. What alternatives are there? What problems have to be solved? What kinds of activity could best be undertaken in large groups and what best in small groups? What other people might be available to help?
2 Discuss the gains and losses if you were to adopt the proposed structure.

If a new structure of the type we are suggesting does prove to be possible, there is, of course, an enormous amount of work to be done. What will this structure allow in terms of the work that children will do? It is impossible to describe this in detail, because so much will depend on what develops in individual schools and this is one of the strengths of an organisational change of this kind. Consider the following account, because it illustrates some of the important points.

Amanda Perkins always arrived at school a few minutes early. It gave her time to play in the playground with her friends and a couple of minutes to check her timetable for the day. She had known it for some time, and it was in any case on the pinboard in the playground and on the 'Notices for Parents' board in the corridor. But like other children she enjoys being able to call it up from the computer especially as she can check the 'expectations for each session' file.

She is pleased she is starting with a large-group session, partly because this includes a video today and partly because she enjoys taking the silent session of 'note making' afterwards; and she has seen that she will spend some of the time continuing with her work on the computer. She has already memorised the standard program and is working on the investigation. But the note making is also enjoyable. She knows that many of her friends make their own notes from the photographs that help them remember the video sequence and the teacher's lesson; but she is still not too good at writing and is making a lot of improvement with the cassette and word choice books she uses. This means that she will get a good set of notes about the Aztecs to use in the lesson on Friday [a small-group discussion session].

As Amanda is putting her notes into the tray for David [this week's monitor] to take back to the base room she realises that she will have to complete hers on Thursday lunchtime, not tomorrow, because of 'recorders'. She would have finished, of course, but for the computer session . . . 'I wonder what I need to do to finish the seven-sided shape?'

She watches David as he takes the box to the base room ready for each of them to file their work, and chats to Tim on the way out to play. Tim is a year younger than Amanda, so although he works with her in the large-group session, they are not in the same base group. Funnily enough, it was for the first

A large group is not something to be regretted ...

time, today, that she realised that when they all watch the same video they have different sheets for note making. It must have been the same for her when she was with the older ones last year. 'In fact, come to think of it, I saw the same video last year but I now have to look for different things.'

The next session is in the small group she works with. This is really good, as it's science. Mrs Palmer starts by using slides to remind them of what they discussed last time, then it is time for the experiments. As usual, there is plenty of space with just four groups of four, with Jamie and Alice working with Mrs Palmer most of the time and the student teacher always ready to help if she needs her.

Jamie is absent a lot and Alice has just come to the school; 'perhaps that's why they don't take part in the presentations at the end of the unit'. So we have got to check that the bulbs are dimmer than that one was in that circuit and explain why. It looks like those electrons again.

'I've got my test after lunch', she remembers. This is the one that she's been working towards to 'get it perfect', and she is now really confident with the protractor, so she should be OK. Then she goes straight into observational drawing, still in the large-group room. This is actually quite hard and she looks forward to doing ceramics or painting that some of her base group are

Amanda calls up her timetable on the computer

doing. Mind you, there is a lot of help available from the student teachers who introduced the work in the first place. It is interesting that they all seem to be good at shading – perhaps that's what you learn when you are a student. It's useful to get all that help: 'I wonder why that university lady told them not to help so much but to "stand back"?'.

School organisation and curriculum detail

This story illustrates a number of points that are related to Unit 3. The work that is done in large-group sessions relates very largely to work with facts and skills as described in that unit. This means not only an introduction to them and the subsequent memorising and practice, but also to the testing of the level of mastery that has been decided is appropriate. The testing that features in the above story has a wider purpose: it lays out for the children the direction in which their work is going, and makes them aware of their use of previously

acquired skills. This only applies if the small-group sessions really do then capitalise on these facts and skills, so this would need to be a priority in planning.

The obvious advantage of a small-group session is the opportunity to pay closer attention to individuals. Any attention that is 'closer' ought to be 'better'. But the important question is how this small-group session can be made really productive. There are many matters that will need attending to, but priority might well be given to what we called 'structured conversation' in the nine dimensions described in Unit 2. Carefully planned to be based on the work from the large-group sessions with which children already have some familiarity, it enables them to understand and apply as yet uncertain knowledge.

The memorisation of facts and the mastery of skills is only a part of 'knowing', and children need to give voice to what they know and what they are uncertain about. The organisational structure described above adds a further element to this, in that it emphasises how 'understanding' begins when facts and skills are being learned, and is best done when the ones that are to be given special attention are clearly signalled. That is one of the purposes of the element of formality that the large-group sessions bring; and it is one of the purposes of the specific testing programme that is implied.

One important feature of Amanda's day described earlier is the reference to working in a mixed-age large group and the use of the same video in successive years for different purposes. This is an obvious use of video. In many cases, video sequences, whether they are designed for schools or taken from normal broadcasting, are so rich in information that they are not only amenable to a second showing some time later, but actually benefit from it (and this is quite separate from any repetition on each occasion).

There are a number of examples in Amanda's story of how specific assistance is given to children in doing their tasks. At one point we see how some children are prompted to recall the content by reference to photographs. Multi-media teaching can be very appropriate to this form of organisation, and it is not necessary to rely on print and the teacher's voice alone. Schools now have access to microcomputers, radio, sound and video cassettes, television, and will in the coming years make use of interactive videodisc and possibly 'virtual reality', the three-dimensional simulation medium.

However, working the way we have described above does not require high technology and expensive equipment, though it does require imagination and initiative, as well as careful planning. We have posed this large-group/small-group proposition, not because it is the only desirable way to proceed, but because it is a useful device for helping a group of teachers think about alternatives to their current practice. Sometimes, in the quest for greater individual and collective effectiveness, it is important to challenge assumptions and practices in a constructive manner. We have offered one avenue for doing this, but there are numerous others.

APPENDIX: THE NINE DIMENSIONS OF TEACHING

The criteria for the nine dimensions of teaching shown below represent progression from relatively simple levels of performance to more complex expressions of competence. As we have said in Unit 2, this is not put forward as a paragon ideal, merely as one way of looking at teaching which shows how teachers can progress. There are seven or eight levels in each case, though dimension 0, ethos, is not expressed in levels.

The first three levels, approximately, illustrate the kinds of work students should be doing at the end of initial training; they also represent what we see as the essential basic teaching skills for the accomplished teacher, as they can be built upon. The achievement of more sophisticated levels is seen in the daily work of some teachers, but on the whole these levels are achieved from time to time as they are judged appropriate. That is to say, they are within the repertoire of the experienced teacher, but are called upon in response to a professional analysis of what is needed.

Although we have indicated that students are able to achieve approximately level three in each dimension by the end of initial training, it is important to recognise that this is variable, and some will achieve far more. The idea is that an appropriate record of what has been achieved is central to further professional development, so that all teachers can develop throughout their career. This, of course, is consistent with many staff development or appraisal schemes that schools already use.

Dimension 0: Ethos

The developing teacher should progressively:

- Show interest in children as people.

- Maintain warm relationships, seek to understand differences in children's personal appearance and habits; hold all children in positive regard.
- Create time for children's interests and conversation and act as a model in encouraging mutual respect.
- Encourage self-evaluation; create or act on opportunities to minimise bias, prejudice or stereotyping; canvass pupils' views and perspectives across the whole class.
- Encourage children's initiative and cooperation; design tasks requiring cooperation; create or capitalise on opportunities for negotiating rules and standards or other matters in personal and social education.
- Teach children self-evaluation and monitoring skills; teach through negotiation of power, authority and responsibility.
- Experiment with approaches to transfer of elements of power and initiative based on teaching children to act responsibly.
- Sustain large elements of a negotiated curriculum, secure in the knowledge that pupils share purposes and values.

Dimension 1: Direct Instruction

1 Attract children's initial interest; maintain appropriate sequence using supplied material for demonstrations and descriptions.
2 For demonstrations and descriptions, organise suitable seating arrangements, introduce material well, use appropriate visual aids, sustain children's interest.
3 Check clarity of explanation by appropriate questions; convey enthusiasm with appropriate verbal and non-verbal behaviour.

4   Choose appropriate examples, analogies and metaphors; explain as well as describe and demonstrate.
5   Choose concepts with both subject matter and children's interests in mind; ensure children's engagement and participation; use a range of examples and aids to meet diversity of children's attainments; summarise key issues.
6   Pace explanation in light of children's responses with regard to interest and comprehension; show grasp of possible content options and justify particular choices.
7   Make explanations efficient and concise; choose examples for their power in the subject.

Dimension 2: Management of Materials

1   Provide and manage materials for an exemplar activity.
2   For an exemplar activity, check availability of required materials; ensure proper use of these; manage appropriate use, including sharing and subsequent collection.
3   Introduce modifications to individual activities to encourage children's role in management of materials.
4   Identify materials needed and resource working for a limited range of activities and time; utilise a variety of resources from a range of sources.
5   Sustain the resourcing across a range of activities; predict long-term needs and requisition appropriately; encourage children's role in selection, organisation and management of materials.
6   Use available materials imaginatively and creatively.
7   Experiment with and use own materials which improve on available items.
8   Design, produce and use novel materials effectively.

Dimension 3: Guided Practice

1   Distribute provided material; check children's responses.
2   Manage provided material; make time to respond to children during work period; check children's work for accuracy.
3   Provide and manage material for small aspects of the work.
4   Respond rapidly; reinforce; check some work of all children; understand how the exercises are sequenced and structured; make time to

question children about their work to assess the effectiveness of the task.
5   Provide a programme of guided practice in core areas of the curriculum to suit range of attainments in class; choose appropriately matched and sequenced practice exercises.
6   Properly use a range of techniques for practice (including games, microcomputers); spot patterns of errors and use this to provide appropriate remedial work.
7   Move children on to independent practice; encourage children to design own practice programmes.
8   Encourage children's self-evaluation through practice; use practice for skill reconstruction as well as skill refinement.

Dimension 4: Structured Conversation

1   Listen carefully to what children are saying and respond supportively.
2   Attempt to elicit children's responses; recognise and attempt to analyse difficulties.
3   Use planned and unplanned opportunities to hold conversations with children to establish their perspectives.
4   Focus on challenging children's ideas by drawing attention to and providing conflicting ideas; by asking for examples and supporting children in reporting their thinking.
5   Experiment with planned conversational teaching on particular aspects of the curriculum.
6   Experiment with small-scale and limited-duration conversational teaching as an occasional feature of the classroom work.
7   Plan for and experiment with conversational teaching in many curriculum areas by maintaining the children's engagement in exploring a variety of directions raised through conversational teaching.
8   Adopt a chairperson's role in fostering thoughtful consideration of appropriate concepts and issues.

Dimension 5: Monitoring

1   Observe children working and intervene to sustain the momentum of the work.
2   Check children can follow and complete the work set.
3   Monitor in order to sustain order and momentum of work; give appropriate feedback; keep simple records of evaluation.

4 Monitor flow of work to sustain availability of resources and ensure efficient transitions; monitor use of time; detect problems of order early; keep thorough records of attainment.

5 Explore children's understanding of work set; make appropriate observations and attempt hunches to explain children's responses; keep records of evaluation.

6 Use monitoring to create hypotheses about children's difficulties; attempt to analyse and test hunches; use monitoring to inform larger-scale adjustments of teaching.

7 Create time for and attempt deeper diagnosis of children's responses to tasks.

8 Sustain a broad programme of diagnostic teaching.

Dimension 6: Management of Order

1 Attempt to operate some procedures for an orderly activity.

2 Attempt to operate an established framework of rules and procedures.

3 Continue with attempts to operate an established framework of rules and procedures.

4 Anticipate problems of order; attempt to meet these with a clear system of rules through explicit teaching.

5 Anticipate the need for and identify own set of rules and procedures; work at teaching these rules and procedures; attempt to secure appropriate role for children; persist in trying to assimilate disruptive children to the class community; use a variety of approaches with disruptive children whilst maintaining a sense of proportion.

6 Broadly succeed in establishing a system of order on the basis of an appropriate system of rules and procedures.

7 Achieve a situation in which order is mainly carried by the work system on the basis of a careful analysis; systematically attempt to develop an appropriate programme for disruptive children.

8 Achieve a situation in which order is endemic to the work system.

Dimension 7: Planning and Preparation

1 Plan basic resources for children working on a given activity.

2 Plan with a clear purpose; indicate materials for teacher and children; recognise practicalities including resources, time and safety; select content to meet purposes.

3 Plan specific activities to engage a variety of identified skills and intellectual processes including enquiring, imaging, connecting, hypothesising, theorising, planning.

4 Plan a short programme of work to engage a variety of identified skills and intellectual processes and demonstrate attention to transition between activities.

5 Plan whole schemes to engage a balance of identified skills and intellectual processes with clear reference to policy guides, continuity and progression and demonstrating a sound grasp of appropriate subject and curriculum knowledge.

6 Plan to allow for imaginative adaptation of ideas to circumstances.

7 Plan for efficiency in use of time and resources with clear reference to the careful management of the teacher's time.

Dimension 8: Written Evaluation

1 Give some account of own performance.

2 Provide valid descriptions of own performance and children's reactions to tasks; offer tentative justifiable analyses, especially with respect to appropriate use of resources and materials.

3 Provide broader-ranging but concise descriptions of own performance and children's reactions, including reference to knowledge, skills and attitudes.

4 Offer alternative analyses especially with respect to appropriate use of resources and materials. Evaluate, albeit selectively, across whole class.

5 Offer justifiable explanations of children's responses to work; use these explanations in practicable ways to plan the next phase of work; show understanding of diversity of pupils' attainments.

6 Systematically evaluate aspects of class work using a broad range of data to check out explanations and challenge assumptions about specific children.

7 Relate evaluations to broader curriculum planning, seeing, for example, the need for re-planning schemes.

8 Reflect on evaluations to reconceptualise personal model of teaching; challenge own assumptions about subjects, curriculum, organisation.

REFERENCES

Alexander, R., Rose, J. and Woodhead, C. (1993) *Curriculum Organisation and Classroom Practice in Primary Schools: A Follow-Up Report*, London: Department for Education Publications Centre.

Ausubel, D.P. (1968) *Educational Psychology: A Cognitive View*, New York: Holt, Rinehart & Winston.

Biddle, B.J. and Ellena, W.J. (eds) (1964) *Contemporary Research on Teacher Effectiveness*, New York: Holt, Rinehart & Winston.

Brown, G. and Wragg, E.C. (1993) *Questioning*, London: Routledge.

Bruner, J.S. (1977) *The Process of Education*, Cambridge, Mass.: Harvard University Press.

Central Advisory Council for England (1967) (Plowden Report) *Children and Their Primary Schools*, London: HMSO.

Department of Education and Science (1975) (Bullock Report) *A Language For Life*, London: HMSO.

Department of Education and Science (1982) (Cockcroft Report) *Mathematics Counts*, London: HMSO.

Department of Education and Science (1988) (TGAT Report) *Report by Task Group on Assessment and Testing*, London: HMSO.

Doyle, W. (1978) 'Paradigms for research into teacher effectiveness', in Shulman, L.S. (ed.) *Review of Research in Education*, Vol. 5, Itasca, Illinois: Peacock.

Dunne, E. and Bennett, N. (1990) *Talking and Learning in Groups*, London: Routledge.

Dunne, R. and Harvard, G. (1992) 'Competence as the meaningful acquisition of professional activity in teaching', in Saunders, D. and Race, P. (eds) *Developing and Measuring Competence*, London: Kogan Page.

Gage, N.L. (1978) *The Scientific Basis of the Art of Teaching*, New York: Teachers College Press.

Gage, N.L. (1985) *Hard Gains in the Soft Sciences*, Bloomington, Ind.: Phi Delta Kappa.

Guetzkow, H., Kelly, E.L. and McKeachie, W.J. (1954) 'An experimental comparison of recitation, discussion and tutorial methods in college teaching', *Journal of Educational Psychology* 45:193–209.

Wragg, E.C. (1993) *Class Management*, London: Routledge.

Wragg, E.C. (1994) *An Introduction to Classroom Observation*, London: Routledge.

Wragg, E.C. and Brown, G. (1993) *Explaining*, London: Routledge.

THE LEVERHULME PRIMARY PROJECT

The Leverhulme Primary Project workbooks on classroom skills, of which this book is an example, include the texts by Brown and Wragg (1993), Dunne and Bennett (1990), Wragg (1993) and Wragg and Brown (1993) cited above, on questioning, group work, class management and explaining respectively. The research findings from the project, based on the analysis of over a thousand lessons in primary schools, as well as on interviews with and questionnaires from both experienced and novice teachers, are reported in the two books below, both of which are published by Routledge:

Bennett, S.N. and Carré, C.G. (1993) *Learning to Teach*, London: Routledge.

Wragg, E.C. (1993) *Primary Teaching Skills*, London: Routledge.